How to Identify & Navigate TOXIC Relationships

You Deserve More

Jill Hartzog, BSN, RN
and
Raymond Aaron

Toxic Relationships: 2nd in the You Deserve More! Series

www.jillhartzog.com

Copyright © 2020 Jill Hartzog

ISBN: 978-1-77277-335-4

All rights reserved. No portion of this book may be reproduced mechanically, electronically, or by any other means, including photocopying, without permission of the publisher or author except in the case of brief quotations embodied in critical articles and reviews. It is illegal to copy this book, post it to a website, or distribute it by any other means without permission from the publisher or author.

Limits of Liability and Disclaimer of Warranty

The author and publisher shall not be liable for your misuse of the enclosed material. This book is strictly for informational and educational purposes only.

Warning – Disclaimer

The purpose of this book is to educate and entertain. The author and/or publisher do not guarantee that anyone following these techniques, suggestions, tips, ideas, or strategies will become successful. The author and/or publisher shall have neither liability nor responsibility to anyone with respect to any loss or damage caused, or alleged to be caused, directly or indirectly by the information contained in this book.

All the stories within this book have been altered to protect the privacy of the individuals involved. All the names have been changed.

Medical Disclaimer

The medical or health information in this book is provided as an information resource only, and is not to be used or relied on for any diagnostic or treatment purposes. This information is not intended to be patient education, does not create any patient-physician relationship, and should not be used as a substitute for professional diagnosis and treatment.

Publisher
10-10-10 Publishing
Markham, ON
Canada

Printed in Canada and the United States of America

Dedication

To those who want the freedom... to breathe.

Dedication

Table of Contents

Foreword ix

Acknowledgements xi

Introduction 1

My Story 3

Chapter 1: The Sandwich Generation 9
    Boomerang Children or Those That Are in
    No Hurry to Leave Home 12
    Working to Make Your Children Independent and Move Out 17
    Caring for Aging or Ill Parents 20
    Advocacy and Consent 23

Chapter 2: Romantic Relationships 33
    Three Phases of Relationships 34
    Signs of a Toxic Romantic Relationship 36
    Remedies for Toxic Romantic Relationships 42

Chapter 3: Toxic Friendships 47
    What Are Healthy Friendships? 47
    How Do You Know it is Toxic? 50
    The Risks of Toxic Friendships 55
    Finding Solutions for Toxic Friendships 56

Chapter 4: Toxic Relationships at Work 61
    The Benefits of a Healthy and Safe Workplace 61
    Types of Toxic Behavior in the Workplace 64
    Improving Workplace Relationships Despite Toxic Elements 70

Chapter 5: Toxic Relationship with Your Mental Health 75
    The Benefits of Stable Mental Health 76
    Understanding Declined Mental Health 78
    Significant Mental Health Issues 78
    Milder Mental Health Issues 80
    Signs of Declining Mental Health 81
    Depression 81
    Anxiety 82
    Poor Self-Care or Self-Sabotage 83
    Emotional Withdrawal 84
    Addictions 85
    How to Improve Your Mental Health 86

Chapter 6: Toxic Relationships with Your Body (Physical Health) 91
    The Benefits of Physical Self-Care 92
    Feeling Happy 92
    Improved Confidence 93
    Improved Relationships 93
    Weight Management 95
    Energy and Memory Alertness 96
    Immune Health and Acute or Chronic Illness 97
    Signs Your Physical Health is Declining 98
    Creating Change to Remake Yourself,
    for Your Best Physical Self 102

Table of Contents

Chapter 7: Recognizing Toxic Social Media,
and Limiting Their Influence 109
    The Benefits of Social Media 111
    The Potential Toxic Aspects of Social Media 113
    Finding Healthy Ways to Limit Social Media 117

Chapter 8: Toxic Strangers 119
    Identifying Potentially Toxic Behaviors 121
    Road Rage 122
    Prevention of Escalation 123
    Verbal and Physical Aggression 124
    Prevention of Escalation 124
    Online Dating 125

Chapter 9: Always Forward, Never Back 131
    Takeaways 134
    Moving Forward 136
    Main Tips 138
    Final Thoughts 140

About the Author 143

Foreword

Throughout your lifetime, you will have countless relationships and encounters with others. While you can have healthy relationships, the challenge is identifying when a relationship is no longer healthy, and how to address it. In *How to Identify & Navigate TOXIC Relationships: You Deserve More*, Jill Hartzog dives into a variety of unhealthy relationships and gives you tools that can help you manage them successfully.

One of the first relationships Jill focuses on is the sandwich generation, where you have to care for your parents, while still caring for your own children. Her knowledge and experience helps you to understand how to better navigate the challenges of this time of life. However, Jill also addresses unhealthy romantic relationships, giving tips to help you identify toxic elements within your romantic relationship.

How to Identify & Navigate TOXIC Relationships, as part of the You Deserve More series, also breaks down the toxic elements that can become part of your relationship with yourself. Jill gets into how you talk to yourself, how you care for yourself physically, and how you care for yourself mentally, thus helping you to understand how you care for yourself directly impacts the other relationships in your life.

Finally, Jill talks about how you process those random negative encounters which happen on a daily basis. Her focus is on stopping the negative energy from these events before it permeates your entire day.

How to Identify & Navigate TOXIC Relationships

Each of the chapters also includes activities and ideas that allow you to take action in your relationships right away.

If you are looking for a guide to understanding toxic relationships and what you can do to create change, then *How to Identify & Navigate TOXIC Relationships: You Deserve More* is a powerful resource for you!

Loral Langemeier
The Millionaire Maker

Acknowledgements

I am truly awed and inspired by the many amazing people I have met throughout my personal and professional life, who go out of their way to make the world a better place for others. My goal is to continue to energize those that want to achieve and accomplish more for themselves and others!

Introduction

Are you, or anyone you know, facing particularly challenging relationship dynamics, ones that are creating additional problems to other aspects of your life? Are you dealing with relationship issues with your parents, siblings, partner, or your own children? Other relationships related to your professional career could also be creating an obstacle for your professional growth. With all this in mind, you might be asking yourself how you can tackle the challenge of a toxic relationship, and what you can do to help yourself. Why is it holding you back from achieving other desired goals in your life?

This book is designed to reach out and share with you the knowledge and tools I have used in my personal and professional life to help people meet the challenges related to toxic relationships. One thing that has become evident throughout the years is that dysfunctional relationships are rarely one-sided, and that there are two or perhaps several people that contribute to these relationship issues, with multiple aspects from their upbringing and life events, which contribute to a person's personality, opinion, and desires.

My goal for you, in writing this book, is to empower you to identify what toxic relationships are, see that you are not alone, and start the process of healing and resolution. Often, individuals may counsel you to end the relationship, telling you to safeguard your emotional well-being. That may be well-intentioned and true, but there are lots of reasons why we continue to put up with harmful relationships—financial dependency, love, expectations, loneliness, guilt, and loyalty, just to name a few. What happens when quickly ending a toxic relationship is not something you *can* do, or something you *want* to do?

Many of us won't want to end a relationship with a family member; we can't just stop talking to our parents, children, or siblings. What if the toxicity is at work? We can't easily quit our jobs without a plan in place for income replacement. However, when it comes to our health and long-term happiness, there is a point where we need to walk away; but first, we want to see if we can work through it. Can we reach a point where the relationship is tolerable? None of this is an easy process, especially when we start to self-advocate and speak up through words or actions. People won't be used to the evolving you—the you who now pushes back and stands up for themselves! Expect some resistance.

Each of the chapters in this book are devoted to the various types of toxic relationships I have seen throughout my life. I want you to realize that you are not alone, and that there are always worse or better situations that others deal with daily.

You will be given skills that you can use to diffuse toxic dynamics within various types of relationships. Remember, my goal is to help you navigate toxic connections in your life, prevent other relationships from becoming toxic, and provide you with the ability to successfully manage them all. Again, I'm not a therapist, and I am unable to provide additional counseling to fix these relationships. When this is required, I do advise seeking out professional counseling! I *am,* however, skilled at empowering and energizing others to be motivated, to make changes, and to move forward.

For more information on how to move forward with personal goals and strategies, please read my book, **You Deserve More: How to Reinvent Yourself at Any Age**, where you will discover what is holding you back, and the steps to move forward, with a plan to achieve them. If one of those is a toxic relationship, then you are in the right place now. Let's move forward and start talking about the different types of toxic relationships people have.

My Story

My journey to understanding and appreciating the complex relationships between individuals started early in my career as a nurse. I have been a registered nurse for over 25 years, working in hospitals and community settings, in both Canada and the United States. During this time, I have encountered many different relationship dynamics, gaining insight and experience on how individuals interact with each other, as well as how they treat themselves.

During this time, I have used this knowledge within my own personal and professional life, helped others gain insight into these connections, helped empower individuals to identify their own goals and desires, and assisted people in creating strategies on how to cope with these relationships. I'm by no means a therapist, and I don't aspire to be one, but I *am* a good listener and have a knack for empowering others to want more for themselves and to seek the means to do so.

In May 1991, I graduated from nursing school, in Ontario, Canada. By October of the same year, I was living in Hawaii while working in the neurosurgical unit at a local hospital. I had always wanted to travel and work abroad, but the extra push started with an emotionally abusive boyfriend that I needed to get away from. I can now recognize how controlling he was, and that he was trying to isolate me from my friends. This man had many issues, not the least of which included an overly inflated ego and a narcissistic personality!

How to Identify & Navigate TOXIC Relationships

In moving from Ontario to Hawaii, I literally crossed the globe to start a new life. I left behind all family and friends, starting over to build new social and professional relationships. Traveling so far away from home also presented a large culture shock, but one that I was determined to learn from and enjoy.

I met so many different people over those years, while working in a large hospital setting—locals from multiple ethnic backgrounds, and various injured tourists from around the world. I also had numerous colleagues who had many different upbringings and cultures, which played key roles in how they formed relationships with others. Adding to this were the challenges of working in a stressful health care environment with acute medical and long-term chronic conditions. I found myself learning and growing while gaining a deeper understanding of all the factors that played into how different relationships formed and carried on. By nature, I'm a people watcher, or people observer, which may be more accurate—and I saw a lot!

It wasn't all amazing though. At times, I had to deal with some deep-seated resentments from island residents, being a Caucasian nurse from Canada. I was considered a "Haole," which means a foreigner, often of Caucasian descent. In looking at the origins of this word, it's been debated whether this word is derogatory or simply descriptive, but it didn't bother me back then, maybe because I simply didn't grow up in Hawaii and was now an adult. However, for the first time in my life, I experienced racism firsthand—sometimes at work, and other times when around the island.

After meeting my new boyfriend, a Navy man who later became my husband, I had to build even more trust from the locals. As a military wife, a common assumption from locals was that I HAD to go to Hawaii, and that my husband had been re-located with no choice. Locals and military have their own dynamics, and it isn't always good. Although, initially, most military families love the idea of moving to Hawaii, after a short period of time, some become quite resentful at being situated so far from home, and they feel trapped on this beautiful island. Locals are rightfully very proud of their islands and heritage, with strong economic ties to tourism and military expenditures, yet also resentful of their presence at the same time.

My husband was in the US Navy and was stationed at Pearl Harbor. Once I became a military wife, I had yet another huge culture to learn and navigate through. During those early years, I ran into men and women who were dealing with long separations from family and friends, having no idea how to care for themselves. Marrying too young when they missed girlfriends back home, then having children before they were even close to being ready—19 to 22 years old—they themselves were still essentially kids. I became a big sister, the professional, someone they could turn to for advice—someone who looked like they knew what they were doing—though I myself was still learning and only in my mid-20s by then.

Basic life skills were virtually non-existent for many of these couples, who often were very poorly educated as well. I remember visiting the homes of some of my husband's married shipmates, seeing food spoiling on the counter, crawling with maggots, simply because they had no idea how to prepare meat safely, particularly in a hot climate. Unlike being stationed on the mainland, where you could drive to see your family or have them come to visit, leaving Hawaii for a trip back home was an expense that few could afford.

Spouses were deployed away for six weeks, or even six months at a time, and mental stress built up. It was not uncommon to find individuals dealing with depression or anxiety from being so isolated. Without the relationship skills to address these issues, I saw young people floundering within their marriages, and feeling so completely overwhelmed. Yes, the military advertises support for families, but I never found it very supportive. Men don't have a say in where they go, what they do, or for how long. Their spouses had to shoulder much of the burden of everyday decisions with finances, home management, single parenthood, and being the *good military spouse*—a very tall order for those so young and inexperienced.

How to Identify & Navigate TOXIC Relationships

When men were away on tours of duty, it became incredibly lonely for many partners. Most of the military wives I knew didn't work. The men themselves missed home and were lonely too, though they formed a tight bond amongst themselves. My military lady friends and I would go out for evenings in Waikiki, which was full of restaurants, shops, and beach walks, but that wasn't really the draw for most. It was to see all the undeployed men that descended on the bar areas from any of the four military stations around the island, and flirt, to feel young and remove some of the stress from their everyday lives.

My husband and I somehow survived those days and stayed true to each other, but I believe there were several factors working in our favor (I had a career that provided decent income, I kept myself busy, and I had built some good friendships at work and via the military). Sadly, we knew that there were many marital relationships struggling and imploding around us.

Emotional needs weren't being met in many relationships, so affairs by women were common—not that it was accepted in any way. When we moved into military housing, one next-door neighbor would actively spy on other wives through her window, watching if men were being brought home when their spouses were away. This caused even worse feelings amongst some of the women, and a truly toxic environment ensued. These affairs were the unspoken reality for many military marriages, and often had tragic emotional and mental consequences for those involved.

As men and their families are often moved to other military stations, we would lose touch but would hear of couples we knew getting divorced years later. We were not surprised.

Over time, I noticed patterns in the relationships of others, and how different challenges created toxicity within any type of relationship— romantic, friends, acquaintances, children, work. Remember, I was continually exposed to a very large turnover of people, both at work and through my personal life; I met an enormous number of people over those years. In my personal life, I was often looked upon as the spouse that knew how to navigate life and the military system, since I had a career and was older than many of the spouses I met.

Throughout my years, friends and new acquaintances have come to me for advice and help, both through my personal and professional life. Somehow, I was able to look like I had it all figured out, even though I didn't think I did; but I've always been a great listener for anyone that had problems to share. Likely that was what people picked up on. I became a mentor, sharing life skills and sometimes a good dose of guidance and direction.

As a long-time health care worker, working at various institutions and work settings, both in hospital and community settings, I had to learn how to navigate many aspects of people's personal relationships and support systems, as well as care for them medically. Home care is not just working with the patient, but also working with their close interpersonal relationships, which impacts how they function and their ability to attain goals. It is not always easy, and those challenges mean that health care workers need to have more than just medical knowledge of the body. They also need to develop some intuitive skills to assist in navigating the emotions of sick individuals, while supporting their emotional and mental health.

Over the years, I have discovered a strong passion for encouraging others to identify their personal wants and needs, then empowering them to make it happen. One recurring theme that holds many people back from attaining them, is when constantly dealing with a toxic relationship. Let's start exploring some of the different types of toxic relationships people deal with.

CHAPTER 1
The Sandwich Generation

Stuck in the middle is exactly what *sandwich generation* means. If you are someone, likely in your 40s–60s, who is both caring for children of any age as well as aging parents, then you are part of the sandwich generation. And if you're a female, statistically you are the likely primary caregiver of both your children and the aging parents in your family.

Being "sandwiched" between these two generations does not in itself mean that the relationships you have with your children and parents are toxic—far from it! The assumption is that most of us want to help both our children and our parents with their wellbeing, ensuring that they are learning or maintaining their independence. A toxic relationship or scenario occurs when this caregiver is not coping, and experiences either of the following increasing stressors:

- Not coping while juggling the responsibility of caring for both children and elderly (and possibly ill) family members, while not taking the much-needed time they need for themselves.
- Working part-time, full-time, or struggling with an inability to work, with resulting financial hardships and costs.

While there will be younger sandwich parents who are caring for young children and ill parents, this group of caregivers is increasingly shifting to the older end of the spectrum. Many will be into their 50s and 60s, as increasing numbers of adult children remain home longer or even return after being away, continuing to require financial assistance. Seniors are also maintaining their health longer, so when they do become ill, they may be well into their 70s, 80s, or 90s, which could leave this sandwich generation as seniors looking after seniors.

When parents become sick, guidance and direction, plus physical, emotional, and/or financial support will be required. This leaves the sandwiched parent/child, who could finally be free to work or enjoy more time with their partner or social groups, with the responsibility of caring for someone again. Added to this, they are themselves aging, likely beginning to deal with their own health issues, and should be actively planning and saving for their own retirement.

Overload, burnout, stress, health and emotional decline—all symptoms and side effects of an unbalanced life, which can lead to emotional fatigue, mental or physical illness, relationship breakdown, or social isolation. How do you have money for a much-deserved vacation, or to socialize with your friends, if you are supporting additional adults on your limited income?

Of course, I think we should help our parents when they become ill, just as we have a duty to teach and support our children until adulthood, but there must be a balance with *YOU* time as well. How can you ever take personal time—take a course, exercise, or enjoy a hobby—if all your free time is consumed with caring for a senior parent? How can you enjoy a stress-free life when you arrive home after a long day at work and find your adult child failing to contribute equally to chores in the family home? Perhaps they have no job, play video games, waste time on social media, and do not help to make or clean up after dinner? How do you think this is going to affect your own health?

There is only so much time in a 24-hour period to juggle many things—something always gives. Sadly, it tends to be the caregiver's health and wellbeing. Juggling our own health needs as a caregiver, while still providing direction and care to an adult child, *and* helping senior family members, cannot be maintained for long.

The Sandwich Generation

The geography of where you live, the level of support you receive from your partner and siblings, and how receptive your parents are to accept help will additionally play key roles in your ability to cope. We'd all like to think we will age slowly and gracefully, that when we eventually require additional care, we will have had time to prepare without burdening our children. Sadly, this is not a reality for many families.

Sudden health decline creates enormous stress in families that more often are living farther apart. Technology is great in giving us easy access to each other through phone or videos, but when someone needs hands-on care, we need to be there to help or organize it, which is not always possible or affordable. Additionally, depending on your relationship with your parents, they may be reluctant to accept this help or alter bad habits that are contributing to their already fragile health.

Had you ever considered that you may be one of those parents who would be still supporting an adult child, well past when they should be taking care of themselves? Maybe you thought they'd be able to help you with things, instead of you helping them? Had you also ever considered that it may be that you would be helping your aging parents at the same time? Or did you think you'd be traveling, relaxing, and winding down a bit from all those busy years raising children? All of us want this time to enjoy life, where you and your partner can enjoy time alone, reconnect, or socialize with friends.

It's all too common for adult children to remain home longer (failure to launch) or return home after university (boomerang kids)—most commonly because of lack of funds, college/university bills, or mismanaged finances. But how can you tell when this return home is appropriate? Or when are you enabling their behavior to lack responsibility and avoid adulthood, allowing your relationship to become toxic, leading to increased stress on everyone?

Let's discuss the different types of relationships each of us may have with our adult children and our aging parents, and how to prevent toxic sandwich environments, or what to do if you are currently in the middle of one.

Boomerang Children or Those That Are in No Hurry to Leave Home

Make your bed, put away your clothes, do your homework, go to bed early—do you remember when this child/parent relationship seemed so easy? So simple? Yet all too fast, each of us will move on from this scenario and must redefine our relationship with our aging children. What will this new relationship be like? While they can be greatly influenced by our teen/parent relationships growing up—everyone can grow from mistakes and move on to a better relationship—nothing needs to remain static.

Relationships that don't constantly contain negativity, controlling behaviors, or unreasonable demands, with love and respect on both sides, will have better success and an easier time transitioning into healthier adult relationships. There will always be difficult teen years while both parent and child are learning their evolving roles; however, teaching, guiding, boundaries, and discipline are all part of being a parent. How you handle this responsibility, or your child's ability to accept their own, can vary greatly.

No one is perfect. Nor are the personalities of all parents or children the same. Ideally, as children grow into adulthood, they have learned independence, are looking forward to moving on with their own lives, and have the maturity to accept personal responsibility for their own self-management. Parents want to share and celebrate this new stage in their child's life, but also regain their own lives by relinquishing the caregiver role and becoming the parent of an independent adult—yet sadly, this is not the reality in some families.

Some children will grow up without learning the skills necessary to support independence, and they will struggle to live their lives separate from their parents. It's a growing trend to find adults in their late 20s, and sometimes much older, still living at home, covered by their parent's income—and not due to any physical or mental health issues. They don't know how to move on to the next phase; they can't afford to live on their own, or they simply don't have the desire to do

The Sandwich Generation

so. Some will return home as "boomerang" kids, with high debt, but if this occurs, it should only be for a negotiated length of time. Is there anything wrong with having to help your adult children stand on their own two feet when they are well out of a reasonable amount of post-secondary school? Simply put, both yes and no. You may be doing them more harm than good unless you learn how to establish clear boundaries.

If you are providing your adult children money to live on, even if they have a job and live rent-free in your home, who are you really helping? They are not learning to budget within their own means, and you are misunderstanding the importance of your role in teaching your children to be self-sufficient. If you have low expectations of them, they will have low expectations of what they should accomplish; and quite frankly, they may take advantage of that situation.

> **INTIMIDATION** – *I can't get him to leave. He does nothing to help around the house, and even leaves old plates of food in his room. I end up just shutting that door—in my own house! He has no job and still plays video games until early the next morning. All he does is argue with me and his father, swearing or trying to bully us. He's a lot bigger than me, taller, and tries to intimidate me. He's even taken money out of my purse. Once he took my debit card and removed money from my account. I didn't even know he had my card, till I went to use it. He didn't care that I was upset. I didn't think, at 29 years old, he would still be living at home. I thought he'd be married with kids, have a good job... I want him out, but he doesn't have any money—I can't just let him end up on the streets. I wish we could just pack up and leave him behind, but I know I wouldn't do that; he's still my son... Some friends have said to call the police to get him out, but what kind of mother would I be if I did that. Literally, some nights, I just stay out late at work to avoid the fights, or close the door to my bedroom and cry. My husband now just avoids the entire conversation.*
>
> *– Linda J.*

How to Identify & Navigate TOXIC Relationships

This is not the situation you ever want to find yourself in. This is a toxic relationship that is affecting the emotional and mental health of both the adult child and the parents. If, however, you had been clear with some ground rules, where they were helping with household chores, paying their own bills, and providing a clear expectation of when they would move out, continuing to live together into adulthood may be acceptable for a short period of time.

There are many reasons adult children don't want to leave home after high school, or they return soon after university: free rent, ready-made meals, a clean home, low expectations of chores, not having to pay all their own bills. Any of these is enough to make a growing number of children want or feel they need to live at home with their parents for much longer than they should. Temporarily returning home after university or college, with set guidelines of roles and responsibilities, is likely appropriate to get them on their own feet. A child who graduates from high school, and immediately enters the workforce, must also have a plan and expectations, which both parent and child agree upon, in regard to when they must be self-sufficient.

This plan must come with the full expectation that this child will be moving out within a reasonable amount of time, and that mom and dad will not continue to care for them instead of saving for retirement and their hard-earned alone time. The toxic relationship occurs when parents continue to be too lenient with their children, fail to set boundaries, and become the built-in maid or butler service to their children. Toxic is when the adult child cannot recognize that they are draining their parent's finances and good intentions unfairly, and don't want to take on the responsibilities of being an adult. Keep in mind, there are many grandparents in this same position, who take in grandchildren to raise—children who must grow up with their grandparents when parents are unable to raise them, related to mental health issues, criminal activity, or death, to name a few. Grandparents do not necessarily have any more effective coping mechanisms than a younger generation; in fact, they may have an even tougher time setting boundaries due to their unique role.

GUILT – *Don't talk too loudly; he's in the backroom sleeping. He dropped out of college a few months ago after he told us he hates school. Our own son died two years ago, and we've been raising our grandson since then. His mother has not been in his life since he was four. He's been so angry and frustrated since his father died. I don't know what to do, and I feel so bad for him. He's only 19 years old and now only has us and his uncles. My other sons don't like how he treats us, but everyone feels so bad for him. I think he just needs time to get over things and figure out what he wants to do—but it's hard. I take most of his frustration because his grandfather has memory issues and can't do much to help him anymore. Yes, he swears at me... a lot. We used to be so close, but I don't know what to do. I'm getting older and have my own health issues now, so I worry about his future.*

– Margaret M.

What about a child that struggles with a learning disability or mental health issues, such as anxiety or depression, that interferes with their ability to be independent? Parents usually do the best they can with the knowledge they likely learned growing up themselves, but it may not be enough. Children may not be coping themselves, and depending on how severe their situation is, you may need to work with outside programs, counselors, or doctors to help them with their struggles and any possible need for medication or additional support.

Alternatively, they may also use guilt against their parents if allowed, something they learn at a young age, and can choose to abuse as they move into adulthood. Parents will struggle with helping these children versus enabling their behaviors, desiring a better life for them, yet being concerned with their ability to be independent and learn from mistakes. Seek out the help you need when trying to help a child with significant anxiety, depression, or other mental health issues.

MANIPULATION – *My son is 25 years old, and he won't stop playing video games. Yes, he has a job, today, but it's part-time, and he will regularly call in sick if he wants a day off. I'm sure* *he's going to get fired any day now. He smokes pot due to his anxiety, which is good, I think. He's had ADHD (attention deficit hyperactivity disorder) since he was young, and he was always the son I had to help more. Marijuana was the only thing that calmed him down as a teenager, though now all he does is smoke pot and game. He stays up late, sleeps all day, and doesn't seem to have a lot of friends—well, except online. He doesn't help in the house at all; and honestly, it's not worth the fight anymore. When I ask him what his future plans are, he gets quiet, defiant, and says that he can't afford to move out—do I want him on the streets? I can't see him ever leaving home. He's only finished high school and has no interest in learning a trade or getting a full-time job. I've helped him so many times to find courses, but he never follows through. How can anyone live off minimum wage and have their own place these days? I feel so bad for him!*

– Anna R.

There are many reasons parents struggle to develop independent children. When we think of the word, *toxic*, abuse or neglect immediately comes to mind when discussing parent/child relationships—but that is not always the case. Families will often have poor functioning or unbalanced relationships when parents or adult children struggle with emotional and mental dysfunction. These children may have unhealthy relationships with their own coping ability, their parents, or siblings, or simply lack the skills necessary to become independent adults. All teens, even adults, will have times of anxiety and depression, but identifying when this person is not developing adequate coping skills is key in preventing future adult issues. Counseling, community resources, and medical intervention must be considered if your child's anxiety is excessive and is interfering with their ability to make healthy decisions for themselves.

While we have put a focus on depression and anxiety, there are many other physical and mental health issues, which do prevent children from *ever* being able to independently care for themselves—each family has their own unique story and situation. Talk to your health care team to determine your best path and need for support.

Working to Make Your Children Independent and Move Out

Self-reflection is key if you find yourself still caring for your adult child past the point that you feel is appropriate, or when you know that boundaries are being crossed. Are you allowing them to use emotional buttons on you, with guilt, fear, or worry? Are you creating this within yourself, instilling your own worries on them, or creating an adult that does not feel they can manage to live on their own and take on adult responsibilities? Is it a combination of both?

It is never too late to backtrack on whatever arrangement, or lack of arrangement, you have with your adult children, to prevent a worse relationship and increased stress in your family. If you expect your children to move back in, for any period, this is when you want to clearly outline your expectations of the relationship from the beginning.

1. Create and sign a clear contract with your adult child, which outlines what your expectations are during their return home. What will they be responsible for related to chores, bills they will pay, meals they will make for the family, and more? After all, they *are an adult* returning to live in your home, not a child you need to continue to care for. Expect them to be actively helping to manage themselves and your home. Picture your adult friend moving in with you temporarily—would you expect them to live independently? Or would you wait on them hand and foot? Don't do more for your children than you would for someone else!

2. If you have not had discussions regarding debt, budgeting, and living within their means, do so now. If you don't know this yourself, seek out professional help for your child, maybe for both of you. Even if there is a cost for a course,

this will provide invaluable education, and save you a lot of money in the long term. Review your child's finances together, and make suggestions on how they can work within a budget to save. If they are living in your home rent-free, don't be concerned that you are invading their privacy with their accounts and finances—make it part of your contract together. They are living with you rent-free! Free utilities, amenities, and food too! A great budget tool, for any age, can be found in my book, ***You Deserve More: How to Reinvent Yourself at Any Age.***

3. Don't be okay with them taking a vacation with friends, buying expensive toys, eating out, and going to the bars excessively—all while living rent-free in your home, and *slowly* paying down their school bills or saving to move out. They should feel poor, they should feel the struggle of paying their bills, and they should be learning to be an *adult* at this age, not extending their years as a child. Think back on how it was when you were growing up. Most of us did not have the same privileges as today's generation, nor the expectation that everything they desire just magically shows up. Teach them that they must earn their ability for such things, and pay for it on their own when they are able to pay for their basic cost of living first. Otherwise, this vacation or toy they have bought is essentially coming out of your pocket, since you are paying their cost of living bills for them while they spend their money on the fun stuff!

4. Don't make life so comfortable for them. Why would anyone want to move out if you do everything for them? Don't do their laundry or make all their meals, never expecting them to have to help with some shopping, cleaning, or home maintenance. Their childhood days are over, and both of you need to accept this. They should always have a clear understanding that this living situation is temporary, and they should want to move out. Deal with any hurt that this may cause you as a parent, and get over it. Our intention

with our children is to make them independent, self-sufficient adults, with their own families, goals, and dreams. Plan to look forward to possible grandparent time ahead instead. As my husband repeatedly says to our adult son, if you don't like the rules, there's the front door. Some of you may think this sounds harsh, but it gets the point across and keeps him on his path when inevitable disagreements come up.

5. Remind them frequently, on a set date you both agreed upon, that they should be moving out. Can this date be changed? Of course, but this is something you discuss together regarding the change in the situation and how to get back on course. It may also depend on how things have been going so far—are they living up to previously defined expectations, and is everyone getting along? Review their savings plan again; are they short on funds for a down payment on a home, or first and last month's rent on an apartment? I'm not opposed to helping them a bit with this if you feel they have been acting responsibly. This may save you more money in the long run, if your adult child is living independently and maintaining their own home instead of living with you for several more years.

6. When an arrangement with your child is not working, or they are not accepting of these rules, what about family counseling? An unbiased third-person perspective may be just what everyone needs. Your child may need to hear from someone else that this situation is not acceptable, that whatever they are dealing with should not be a reason to remain at home. This may also help you understand and accept some responsibility for your own actions, or inactions, in this situation. Have you done anything to enable this situation with your child to reach this point? How can you learn to follow through with what needs to now occur? Do they use guilt and sympathy against you? Expect this to get worse initially, and learn to get tough.

7. Has this toxic situation evolved to the point where your child is aiming threats of physical abuse against you? Threatening their safety or your own? If it gets to this point, you need to seek medical attention or get your local police involved with this eviction process. Consider your child a non-paying tenant in your home, and understand that everyone has the right to live in safety. Consider also how this type of stress is affecting your health, and get the support you need from other family and friends, in order to follow the next steps, with the process appropriate for your situation.

Caring for Aging or Ill Parents

It's not always noticeable when our parents start to age, especially if you live nearby and are in regular contact together. It's not something any of us wants to deal with, yet it is the natural progression of life and will affect us all at some point. How can we best plan for this eventuality, and what do we do if suddenly we find ourselves in this caregiver role? Is there any way to prepare for this? How do we start this conversation with our parents and siblings when some family members don't feel comfortable with this discussion?

Your future planning conversations do not literally just have to be about death and dying; you should also incorporate discussions on what your parents' future goals are. Is there anywhere they'd still like to travel, anything they'd still like to see? Get to know your aging parents better, and understand their plans. Why? This will help you in the future when you, siblings, or other family members want to help or guide your parents with any assistance. Knowing what their beliefs and wishes are will help everyone feel good about future decisions regarding care and illness.

There are many things that we can do to prepare ourselves, our siblings, and our parents for the future. Being on the same page, or relatively so, will prevent a lot of stress, financial hardship, and arguments in the future. Let us first discuss how to prevent the toxic breakdown of these relationships, and see how we can best prepare for this, prior to any ill health of the seniors in our families.

1. Get to know how your parents envision their future: What do they want to do? Where do they see themselves living? What else is important for them to see, and is there anything they still want to do or try? This is likely also going to turn into a really nice conversation. We often forget to ask our parents about their opinions and future goals, when we ourselves get busy with our own families.

2. What are their finances like? I know this is a hard conversation to start—our parents are used to being in charge and may not want to disclose very much, but having a basic understanding of where they are financially is very important. Did your parents pay off their mortgage? Do they have any large bills they are still paying down? Do they have any savings? Can they afford to hire private assistance for themselves, or to manage their home in the future (grass cutting, cleaning, meal preparation, personal care)? Would they consider selling their home to move into a retirement home in the future, so no one needs to worry about managing those things?

3. Who in the family would they want to appoint as their Power of Attorney (POA) for health, and who for finances? There is no rule for who they choose, nor that they must pick the same people for both health and finances. Often, couples choose their spouse first, then one, all, or a combination of their children second—but it doesn't have to be this way. Your parents should select family members or friends that they feel will best represent their wishes if they were unable to make decisions for themselves.

4. Are there one or more family members who would best perform the role of primary caregiver for your parents? Someone who could step up to provide more physical assistance or be available to organize care, be involved in care

meetings, or take them to doctor appointments? Various activities should be divided by different family members to prevent one person from burning out. Additionally, those who provide physical care or live with your parents should not also be the only ones completely shouldering financial costs. What can other family members do to ease the burden of the main caregiver(s) so that everyone feels they are contributing?

5. Have a copy of important documents, like their POA for health and finances, available so that no one is scrambling to find these when needed. This may include documents related to a cemetery plot, life or disability insurance, or any benefits that may pay for equipment or other items they need.

6. Know where your parents have a list of their medications, diagnosis, and doctors, so you can access this if someone requires hospital care. If you are the main caregiver and already involved, you should already have this list. In fact, at any age, this is a good idea for us all to have written down so that partners can also have this available if we become ill. Being prepared decreases future stress and potential arguments within a family left trying to sort things out after the health decline of a loved one.

The above suggestions are all great if everyone has the chance or agrees to pre-plan; however, it doesn't always go this way or proceed in an orderly fashion for many families, for a variety of reasons. The most notable reason is that if you have high functioning and healthy parents, it can happen more quickly than expected. It always seems too early to have this conversation, and some people are in denial or are unwilling to engage in this conversation. It may also be because siblings have moved away from each other, so the only time everyone is together is during the holidays or special occasions—which never seems to be the right time to talk about illness, debility, or death.

Not all families get along well or are willing or even capable of preplanning their own lives, far less working with siblings and their own parents to help plan for theirs. You can imagine that arguments and discord occur when illness befalls a parent, and all children only then begin to discuss options, especially if siblings didn't all get along well up to this point.

Additionally, if you are the child that has been most recently involved in your parent's life, and a sibling shows up to make demands or issue directives, you can expect some conflict. That doesn't mean they don't have the right to an opinion and that you shouldn't work together, but they need to also be respectful of your role as well. If you've already been acting as the main caregiver for the aging parent, you likely know much more about their condition and care requirements. Know that you are all trying to follow your parent's wishes to the best of your ability. With a POA already in place, if your family member becomes incapable, this document will ultimately determine who will be making health and financial decisions for them, regardless of what other family members may want.

Toxic sibling relationships that involve aging parents can become a power-play between these individuals, which can spill over to affect the health of the patient, not to mention the health of yourself and your sibling.

Advocacy and Consent

As a health care provider, my job is to help patients with their wishes for care and treatment, and to help support the family unit as best as I can. A capable adult, regardless of age, is able and allowed to make decisions for themselves. This seems to come as a surprise to the adult children of many seniors, who don't understand that they can't tell their parents where they should live or what they should be doing. Capable adults can make decisions for themselves, regardless of age or even if there is a risk for an injury, such as a fall, or health decline.

Just because your parent is getting older doesn't mean adult children get to take over.

> **UNAWARE** – I want to put my parents in a nursing home; can you help me do that? No, I haven't talked with them; I don't really want them to know. I know they will say no, but I'm worried about how they are living. What do you mean I have to get their consent? It will only become a fight. Can't I just put them on the list for the far future just in case? We don't need to tell them.
>
> – Chuck G.

The answer to the above question would be a very strong no. No one can make decisions for another capable person on where they will live—not their spouse, not their children, nor their extended family. I have seen ageism (discrimination on the grounds of a person's age) so many times in my career, with children who just assume that at some point in time, they automatically have the authority to direct their parents as they grow older.

At times, I can completely understand why adult children want to do this—they are concerned with their parent's health or other risk factors in their lives. However, that is not always the case, and I have also come across families that have adult children *not* acting in the best interest of their parents' health needs or wishes. There are different types of capacity assessments, and different people who can assess someone's capacity for health, property, and where they wish to live. Overall though, people are always assumed to be capable of making decisions for themselves, unless it has been assessed to be otherwise.

Parents may be showing memory decline and becoming forgetful of doctor appointments, or forgetting to take their medication—but again, this does not mean they are incapable of making general decisions for themselves. Instead, other methods can be set up to help bolster their memory, such as providing a calendar, putting medication in a pill organizer or blister pack that their pharmacy provides, and setting up social programs or hobbies that promote or maintain memory function.

A **Capacity Assessment** is the formal assessment of a person's mental capacity to make decisions about property and personal care. Many situations require capacity assessments to be conducted by specially qualified assessors who must follow specific guidelines. *"When it comes to making a specific decision, capacity is not an abstract concept. The person whose decision it is must assess the patient as being able to understand the information relevant to that decision, and must be able to appreciate the reasonably foreseeable consequences of that decision."*[1]

If you are seeking more information on capacity, check online with the website for your local Attorney General or healthcare agency. You can alert someone of your concerns with someone's capacity, and find information on health and financial POA, guardianship, the different types of capacity assessments, and guidelines for different needs. Additionally, some countries have specific health assessors who can determine a patient's ability to make the decision for long-term care admission alone. Look into your local home care services for further questions.

The dynamics of family relationships are nothing short of complex. No two families are the same, with interwoven history and challenging personalities—especially as family members age and roles change. The situation then becomes even more complicated as new people join your family unit, and roles and responsibilities change yet again when different upbringings are added to the mix. Relationships that have a good foundation can usually sustain fluctuating stress levels in the family. Those that have fragile bonds likely won't endure, and toxic relationships can form or expand. Never is that more obvious to me, as a community health nurse, than when a family member becomes ill and everyone has their own differing opinions and suggestions.

---

1 Jeffrey Cole, N. D. (2010). Assessing Capacity for Admission: A Training Manual for Evaluators. Retrieved from Legislative Assembly of Ontario: http://www.ontla.on.ca/library/repository/mon/24004/300799.pdf

Working in health care, I often find myself trying to walk a fine line—navigating between the needs and rights of my patients, and trying to work together with their family members. Nurses that work in hospitals see a small snapshot of the dynamics at home, if any at all. Nurses who work in community or public health sector, schools, retirement or nursing homes—well, they see a whole different side of how a family interacts, and we well know how family dynamics play a huge role in the wellbeing of an individual.

> **ANGRY** – I got kicked out of my mother's place last month by my stepfather. He had no right to do that, so I called the police on him. Nothing happened though; I just went home. They've been married for 13 years, but things are getting worse for them. They both have memory issues, and he doesn't take good care of her. She has a lot of health issues, and falls all the time, but he goes out and sees his friends. She's always alone, and I really think it's neglect; she's 73 now! She won't listen to me anymore, and I don't even want to visit. I hate seeing her in that apartment, which is so crowded and messy. There isn't any place left to sit down; all the surfaces are covered with stuff, and I know she's a hoarder.
>
> – Ronald A.

The reality is that family members don't always agree with another family member's lifestyle, whether they are healthy or instead become frail and ill. They may really want to help, and think they are doing the best for them, but they are still imposing their beliefs on how someone should live. This is difficult for anyone to come to terms with, since everyone literally lives differently from each other.

When patients do not want to follow safety suggestions made by their health care team, health care workers instead need to ensure people have the right information to make informed decisions, and that they have the capacity to make these decisions for themselves. Family members may not be happy with someone who pushes aside services or safety recommendations, but all capable people have the right to make their own decisions. Additionally, keep in mind that there is a large population of siblings who care for other disabled siblings—with quite similar caregiving issues as those that care for ill parents, aunts, and uncles.

> **MANIPULATION** – *I can't go over to see my mother all the time. She calls me 3–4 times per day, and I don't answer it sometimes, because I'm tired of hearing her cry or complain to me about something else. There's always something she's not happy with. My mother has been a widow for 15 years now, but she still cries about my dad's death like he died this year. I know she has some depression, and I feel bad for her, but she's on medication, and it's more than that. My mother has always had a knack for making me feel guilty. She's never happy with what I buy for her, wants one more item as soon as I shop, and is constantly calling because she wants something done in her apartment. She talks behind my back to my sisters, telling them I haven't done anything for her, even though I see my mother five days a week and am the only one that lives close by. She's driving me crazy and won't listen to the doctor and stop eating salt, even though her blood pressure is sky-high. When I try to talk to her about it, all she says is that she knows she doesn't have much time left (she's 72!), and will likely be dead soon anyway. Why was I trying to take away pleasure from her life, when she has so little?*
>
> *– Janice L.*

At what point do relationships become toxic? When are discussions, arguments, and support needs or demands creating a toxic environment—one that will affect the health of the patient and/or caregiver? Do parents manipulate their children or use emotional blackmail to get their children to do something for them? Will siblings who are arguing with each other criticize or disregard the other sibling's feelings? Some of this is normal during stressful times, and of course, it's easy to have small arguments, but when it becomes excessive, when it's draining, and it affects our personal emotional or physical wellbeing—it's becoming toxic.

It is very important for me, regardless of who I'm talking with, to not label a situation or make personal judgments without getting all the sides of the story and information from those involved. There are a lot of issues between siblings, or between a parent and child, where one is blaming the other or accusing them of specific negative behavior. However, when you ask more questions, you may find that it's not as it was originally portrayed. It is easy to be influenced to a greater extent by the more vocal family member. Always keep in mind what everyone's main focus should be: the well-being and wants of the patient. Don't get pulled into family drama, even if it's your own. If it hasn't been sorted out up till now, it's unlikely to get fixed now with the declining health of a family member! Focus on the patient's needs instead.

Siblings who have had long-term toxic relations with each other, and now need to deal with ailing parents, become some of my most difficult family meetings to conduct. Years of discord have built their negative opinions of each other, and my job is not to fix that discord but to see if people can work well enough together to help achieve the final goal—care for their ill family members.

> **BULLY** – My brother has always lived with Mom; he never moved out and got his own place. My sister and I moved out in our late teens; we couldn't wait to leave that house! My brother was just like my dad—a bully who always made it hard for my sister and me, with everything. I fought with my brother often, always with threats and then fists. My father died 10 years ago; he was not a nice guy. I used to think that I at least got along with my mother, but I came to realize she favored my brother. I don't know why she always took care of him; he didn't deserve it. Even now, with my mother being 82, up till the last few years, she was still giving him money and has created the loser he is today. She now has advanced dementia and is very confused, but I know he's still using her money. I've told the bank several times that my brother financially abuses her, but she put him on her account, and he has access to everything. He's never really had a real job. I don't know

what to do. I don't think he's taking good care of my mother now that she's sick. I literally just push my way in the home, just to be able to see my mom.

— Laura C.

What options do siblings or other family members have when abuse is suspected? What types of abuse are there? What can be done?

- Financial (misuse of funds or assets without consent)
- Emotional (diminishing self-worth, dignity, manipulation and constant criticism)
- Sexual (sexual behavior or intent without consent)
- Physical (physical harm or discomfort)
- Neglect (deliberately or ignorantly withholding basic necessities of life)

Educate yourself on resources in your area. There are various support agencies available, no matter where you live, that can help direct and guide people who you suspect or indicate to you that they are being abused. Escalation to local police, and in many areas law enforcement that works specifically with seniors and disabled adults, may be required in some circumstances, depending on the type of abuse being alleged.

There are many ways to help protect seniors from the risks of abuse, fraud, or neglect.

- Stay involved with your senior relative, even if you live farther away. Know who is in their life.
- Help them stay involved with community activities and social opportunities, and encourage friendships to prevent isolation and depression.

How to Identify & Navigate TOXIC Relationships

- Be involved when they make large financial decisions, to decrease the risk of being taken advantage of.

- Talk to family members about scams and educate them never to reveal personal information or credit card numbers over the telephone.

- Assess and ensure that they have their basic needs being taken care of, by family or paid caregivers.

- Ensure that family members, who are the main caregivers, have the support they need. Being overburdened can make that family member the perpetrator of abuse even when intentions are good.

- Seek professional or legal assistance when abuse is suspected. Banks, lawyers, and police can be notified when any type of abuse is suspected, and assistance needed.

Does the senior you suspect of being abused or neglected have good insight and judgment on the situation, and understand how to get help? Working with an incapable senior who is no longer able to make good decisions for themselves will also complicate matters if prior wishes were not discussed or documented legally. Know who is legally able to make decisions on the part of the senior—was a Power of Attorney completed? If not, the decision-making hierarchy is available online; and without a legally appointed substitute decision-maker, a spouse is first, then all children are equal and must make decisions together.

When families or children cannot agree, however, it can become quite difficult for everyone involved, as all parties have an opinion. There may be additional cultural components that can impact the decisions of various members of the family, which may conflict with the wishes of other family members. Navigating all of these can require good listening skills and open communication.

In any relationship with an aging family member, child or parent, prevention of a relationship becoming toxic and affecting everyone's health is key. Know the signs of emotional and physical fatigue in order to prevent the health decline of everyone involved. See what you can do to prevent toxic relationships with your children or parents, so that you don't find yourself being a non-coping sandwich parent or child. Take steps to prevent or decrease toxicity and the creation of bad situations.

Throughout this chapter, my goal was to show the types of toxic relationship dynamics that can occur within a family when you are acting as a caregiver sandwiched between your adult children and aging parents. Now, let's shift to another type of relationship where toxic elements can negatively impact the health of all individuals involved—romantic relationships.

CHAPTER 2
Romantic Relationships

We all want to fall in love and have that *perfect* relationship—one we all, at some point, have envisioned for ourselves. From a young age, there are dreams about the future, romance, and that perfect partner to share life experiences with. When a relationship becomes difficult and negative, we may not be willing to accept that things have turned out poorly, and unwilling to accept that something needs to be done. While falling in love may have been relatively easy, cutting ties from a relationship turned toxic will prove much more difficult. Being in love is addictive—we all desire pleasure, security, and acceptance. Our tendency is to remain in the fantasy of this relationship, believing it is better than it is, often not wanting to give up easily.

Clearly, there are often many hopes and dreams attached to any relationship, and so much time and effort likely invested. You find yourself imagining life with this person as the level of friendship and intimacy increases. You may even have envisioned creating a perfect life together.

The initial stages of any relationship can be an amazing time, but how do you know it is evolving into something that is good for who you are as a person long term. It is important to not get swept up in wanting love over truly having that deep connection with someone that deserves your love. Do you want to be with this person? Do they make you happy? Do you consider their feelings above your own, and do they do the same to you? Do you both want to help, protect, and be with that other person? Are you able to work through the up and down days of any normal relationship, so that you neither feel neglected, ignored, or bullied? If you are both happy in your relationship, then it may be heading in a good direction; but what if you don't frequently feel this way, and have concerns? How do you know if you are in a toxic relationship or if it is evolving to become one?

When romantic relationships have high levels of toxicity, they become detrimental to the health of those involved. Does that mean couples should not try and work through difficulties and arguments, personality clashes, and unkind behavior? It will depend on that couple's personalities and the bond they share, their willingness to change, and their underlying love and respect for each other. There are many levels of toxicity, and the ability for anyone to change *is* possible, but you both must agree to work through issues. It may also depend on what level of toxicity your relationship is experiencing.

There is always a time that any relationship can evolve, grow, and change for the better. There is also a time where nothing can help it, and the dissolution of this union is in the best interest of both parties, including any children within this family. Let's talk first about the three main stages of romantic relationships, and the progression of normal relationships.

Three Phases of Relationships

All relationships start in the **Passion Phase,** the one that everyone loves. Love is in bloom, and feelings of excitement are evident every time you see one another. You look at your partner with rose-colored glasses, so happy you found each other. You see everything that is wonderful, not noticing bad habits you don't like, and glossing over any troubling areas that may signal incompatibility. You might also be changing your own personality just to impress that other person.

During this period, we feel "high" on love, and become addicted to this feeling—we don't know how we ever existed before this person. We want to feel this amazing all the time, and enjoy it for as long as possible. Over time though, things settle, and other feelings begin to push in. We've reached that point in the relationship where this perfect person, one that we thought was ideal, starts to show some tarnish. Different aspects of their personality become more evident, and you wonder if they hid them from you or how you never noticed them before.

The **Reality Phase** hits when you both start to realize you each have faults. Not everything is always sunny, so you must learn how to work through challenges and personality clashes together. Everyone has different upbringings, ideals, and dreams that are not the same, but can they mesh to form a solid and complimentary long-term bond? The reality phase is when you start working together and compromising on conflicting habits so that things can still get done. It is that time of the relationship where you learn how your significant other can provide the support that uplifts and enriches you as a better person. It is also the time you will notice if they are not making you feel good about yourself. Are they bringing any baggage from their family or previous relationships, and how will this affect the both of you?

The **Acceptance Phase** of a romantic relationship is when you figure out whether you can work together to address the challenges of your relationship. Can your personalities weave to create something more effectively together than apart? You may see that your relationship has toxic elements during this last stage. At this point, you need to make the decision to work on issues with your partner, or decide to get out of the relationship altogether. The initial honeymoon stage is over, and you can see the other person more clearly, but what you do will depend largely on your communication skills, self-confidence, and love for yourself. For many individuals in romantic relationships, deciding whether to work through difficulties or to separate is incredibly difficult, causing strain on your emotional and possible physical wellbeing. Additionally, you need to factor in at what level your relationship contains toxic elements, and how severely it is affecting you. Can you work together, not singularly, to help this relationship become healthy?

What are some of the signs of a toxic relationship?

Signs of a Toxic Romantic Relationship

Immaturity, ego, unrealistic expectations, high stress in a union due to internal or external factors - there are too many reasons relationships begin to fail, and couples find themselves unable to work through difficulties. How individuals cope with obstacles in life, and their general coping skills, will impact relationships and influence how they react in a variety of situations.

There are numerous types of toxic elements that can occur within romantic relationships, and each of them brings their own challenges. Some can be more easily addressed and worked through; others will require more investment and professional intervention. The manipulation of a partner, for one's own gains, is high in toxic romantic relationships. Many relationships will break up permanently if the coupling is creating negative emotional, mental, and physical impacts on either person. Sadly, some will endure, to the detriment of one or both partners' wellbeing.

Poor Self-Confidence – If you enter a relationship with poor self-confidence, then you are less likely to know when and how to place boundaries regarding how you are to be treated by your partner. Even if you know what boundaries should be there, you are less likely to enforce your wants or enforce consequences for violating them. Essentially, your partner can do what they want, and you accept it because you believe their wants and needs are more important than your own. Emotional stress, with anxiety or depression, is likely in this unequal relationship.

Narcissistic Behavior – This type of behavior is often focused on making your partner feel small and unworthy. One partner has an inflated sense of self-importance, and craves a constant sense of admiration from those around them. While it might appear that they are confident and believe in their superiority, the reality is that they are not, and any criticism is often met with an angry or defensive response. A narcissist is likely to engage in games of manipulation, and direct the cause of problems onto their partner instead of acknowledging their own contribution. This partner may always feel that they are right, know more, and need to have the very best. They may only appear to care if you are fulfilling their needs or serving their purposes. This partner's ego drives their wants and needs, and like most toxic relationships, it's an unequal partnership.

> **SELF-IMPORTANT** – *He's right, I've never been that smart; I didn't do well in school, so why do I think I'm capable of going back to school now? He'd have to watch the kids when I'm at school and at work—getting up early. He's not an early person, and struggles to get the kids going in the morning. I know my parents can be hard to take, and they are especially hard on my husband. They don't like how he treats me, but I don't see anything bad—marriages aren't perfect. Sam lost his job a few months ago but says that he will get another one quickly, as he's such a good salesman and knows computers. He just needs the time to figure things out, and I will support him with that.*
>
> *– Kimberly L.*

Hostility – Verbal aggression in a relationship can often be associated with a bullying mentality. Your partner is tearing you down by interacting with you from a place of anger, causing you to feel as if you are walking on eggshells to avoid making your partner upset. No matter how carefully you interact, they still talk to you in a disrespectful way, alone or in front of others. There may be an effort to deliberately hurt you, using cruel teasing, vicious talk, name-calling, threats, withdrawal of affection, and more. All of it ends up representing a need for control through verbal intimidation.

Judgment/Criticism – None of us like to be judged and criticized, but it is worse when your partner does it. The constant use of judgment or negativity ends up breaking one partner down, impacting their sense of self-worth. Eventually, you start to doubt your ability to do anything without your partner's advice or consent, asking them to openly correct you and how you act or appear. This behavior will take a large toll on someone's emotional well-being and self-confidence.

> **CRITICAL** – *I know he won't like what I picked to wear; I'm not even sure why I did it. He always thinks I don't know how to dress, never liking my clothes. I was so embarrassed last week when he made fun of my favorite floral top—he told our friends that I dressed like an old lady. Why does he always want to embarrass me? Tonight, I took my time, and put on heels. What's wrong with high heels? It's not my fault he's only 5' 7"—why do I always need to wear flats? I hope he's wearing his brown shoes—they are higher. I didn't see what he wore out to work this morning... I just caught his eye as I walked into the restaurant. I can already tell that he's annoyed and unhappy with my outfit.*
>
> *– Cindy H.*

Feeling Drained/Depressed – Are you in a relationship where most conversations end up making you feel drained or sad? Is it something that you feel is due to this other person, or an internal battle that you are bringing to the relationship, fighting your own thoughts? Are you supporting and lifting each other up emotionally so that you both feel accepted and understood? Does your partner try to understand your needs and who you are, or do they try to change you, which leads to arguments and stress? Depression is common with any toxic relationship, and it can occur here as well. Identifying what is making you feel bad, and whether it's within you or due to your relationship, is the key to moving forward.

Mutual Avoidance – When you enter a romantic relationship, you want to spend time with that individual because it contributes to the joy you find in life. Alternatively, mutual avoidance is when both of you go out of your way to minimize the amount of time you spend together. One partner may initiate avoidance as a form of distaste or punishment, versus both partners drifting apart over time and spending increasingly less time together. Staying away from each other, always being in separate parts of the house, going to separate social events and on separate vacations, and avoiding any real or meaningful conversations, indicates difficulties within your relationship. Sex also is likely non-existent.

Envy/Jealousy – The most negative aspect of jealousy is the fact that it can make you hound your significant other, making them feel hunted or controlled. It tends to turn individuals into very domineering and controlling partners. The other possibly quite innocent partner is then turned into someone who tries to hide activities and conversations, just to have some semblance of freedom. When this partner tries to pull away, it tends to aggravate the other with more jealousy, turning the relationship into a vicious cycle of controlling and rebellious behaviors. Envy within a relationship means that you can't be happy for your partner's success, and are constantly finding ways to tear them down. Eventually, a relationship cracks because of a lack of support and the constant focus on competition and who's doing better in any aspect of life.

> **ENVY** – *It's so wonderful to be finished my 4 years at university; I can't believe I'm off to teacher's college in September, and one day I will really be a teacher! It's bittersweet though, as my boyfriend—although I know he's happy for me—got me this really nice necklace but seems to be upset with all the attention I've been getting from friends and family. I worked so hard, and my grades were good; I don't want to feel like I should hide my success. My friends who graduated wanted to go away for a girl's weekend—it was only three days, but he didn't like those plans. I decided I wouldn't go; it's not worth the arguments sometimes. I just wish he could be happy for me. I mean, I supported him when he finished his schooling.*
>
> *– Carmen S.*

Lack of Trust and Honesty – When two people are in a relationship, trust is key to building affection, love, and a long-term supportive relationship. A lack of trust is often built upon circumstances where one partner feels betrayed by the other, even if that was not their true intention. Honesty is a building block for a healthy relationship, but if one partner feels that they need to hide information or tell lies, then the other partner will see this lack of honesty as a betrayal. This lack of trust may be towards many things—hiding a bad habit your partner said they stopped, telling someone else intimate secrets you both agreed to keep private, spending money you agreed to save—literally anything that is against the dynamics or an agreement made within your relationship.

Affairs/Cheating – When one partner steps out of an exclusive relationship to pursue someone else, either for a short-term or ongoing affair, this is generally considered the ultimate betrayal in any relationship. Unfaithful behavior can be either physical, sexual, and/or emotional in nature, with the resulting toll being devastating to that partner being cheated on. Many relationships will not survive the betrayal of an affair, and those that do can almost always have ongoing trust issues.

> **DECEITFUL** – *I know it's wrong—yes, I do—but I married my husband too young, and it hasn't been fun for a while. You know what it's like when they are away on the boat so long... the Navy doesn't care about us wives left behind, and I know he's going to strip clubs with the guys while away. I'm only 26 and still want to have fun. What's wrong with me feeling love again? He's such a nice guy and so cute! Sex is incredible! I know it's not going to go anywhere; I know that. He's not going to get a divorce either; we just want to have some fun right now. I know you won't tell anyone, but I needed to talk to someone.*
>
> *– Danielle F.*

Physical Abuse – When a relationship becomes physically abusive, there is often any number of other toxic behaviors that are occurring

Romantic Relationships

simultaneously, including mental, emotional, financial, and/or sexual abuse. People in this type of relationship are dealing with much more than bruises and threats—intimidation, isolation, and control exerted over the other partner is occurring. This type of relationship may not occur suddenly; it can evolve over time, with escalating controlling and possessive behaviors. Fear is high for the abused partner, with risks to themselves or involved family members. Having to avoid antagonizing the abusive partner is not a solution, as there may be no reason, even in the abuser's mind, for what triggers aggressive behavior. It is hard to stop when someone escalates to this level of violence, and impossible for the partner to please this person, who can become frustrated due to any number of irrational reasons. The abused spouse, even after they leave this type of relationship, may deal with lifelong effects from it—chronic pain, sexual dysfunction, altered sleep patterns, post-traumatic stress disorder, and low self-esteem, to name a few.

Substance Addiction – For the person that has an addiction, any amount of feelings may be going through their mind: shame, depression, frustration, and self-imposed isolation. Hopefully, your partner is looking for help and is willing to work through the steps to conquer their addiction. It is not uncommon or even unexpected that a partner would want to try and help their loved one. What is often forgotten in this relationship dynamic is that the partner is often so focused on dealing with the actions of their partner, they don't realize the detrimental effects that are also occurring to themselves. How are you emotionally being impacted by your partner's choices? It may be quite similar to what the person with the addiction is feeling—shame, depression, isolation, keeping themselves away from friends and family—but for different reasons.

When someone is addicted to a substance, they become addicted to how that substance makes them feel—it's providing a form of pleasure that the addicted person wants to pursue again and again. The addicted person's brain is not functioning rationally, and they become fixated emotionally and/or physically on regaining that feeling, often at the expense of any relationships in their life. Even if the addiction can be dealt with to the mutual satisfaction of both partners, trust may always be an issue, and an unhealthy dynamic can be created between the couple—much worse if this addiction continues and professional help is not being sought out.

There are numerous different signs in toxic relationships, but what is common in all of them is a loss of trust in the relationship, a lack of mutual respect, and an unequal partnership. One partner may find themselves taking the backseat to the dominant partner, and over time feel resentful and begin to withdraw. If you have identified toxic elements in your relationship, you must make the decision of whether you wish to continue working to improve this relationship, or consider ending it.

What are your next steps to help or end a toxic relationship? Not everything will work in all situations. What are you willing to work through? What is safe to try versus asking for help from friends, family, or professionals, to get the additional support required instead of trying to fix things alone.

Remedies for Toxic Romantic Relationships

During my many years in nursing, the evidence of couples attempting to function within toxic relationships has always been obvious and difficult to watch—and not everyone wants help. Young and old, with various levels of education, or differing religions and ethnicities, toxic relationships are everywhere, and at all different degrees of dysfunction. Let's be honest; there isn't any relationship that can't benefit from more open communication between partners, as everyone will have times of frustration or annoyance with each other. Accepting that this is inevitable, and helping your relationship early when disagreements and discord arise, will prevent toxicity from growing.

Recognize that a big part of addressing the toxic aspects of a relationship involves the willingness of both partners to work on improving this relationship. If only one partner is willing to be involved with change,

Romantic Relationships

the progress of this couple will be quite limited, and it will not bode well for the long-term health of the relationship.

Please note – *If you feel that your physical safety or emotional sanity is at stake, this relationship requires professional help immediately. You should not try to self-help this relationship; instead, leave this environment, and take any at-risk family members with you. Ask your friends or family for help, and contact any local agencies or police in your area that help partners of domestic abuse. These agencies, with various phone numbers per country, can be easily accessed online. The following steps are for relationships you wish to improve and are safe in trying to do so.*

The following steps can be helpful in trying to work on and improve a toxic relationship:

1. Understand yourself and what you want for *you*. This may be harder than you think if you've not been putting yourself first for a long while. Is this a relationship that you want? Is this relationship enriching you? Has it ever? Saying you love someone, blindly, is not enough. Do you think this other person can have an equal partnership with you? Know yourself and what you want first. Right now, at this point, if you decide you no longer want this relationship, it's time to break up and make yourself the priority. Self-heal and take some non-relationship time to figure out who you are and what you want for yourself, and what you want from a future partner.

2. Is the relationship worth working through issues? Start with opening communication with your partner. Do you both acknowledge that there is a problem that needs to be addressed? Do you both want the same thing? Moving forward, partners need to acknowledge the toxic elements in their relationship in order to be able to work on healing and repairing their union. Going forward, there is no more *you*; there is *us,* working through issues *together*. If you are

not both on board with repairing your relationship, there is no ability to mend this partnership.

3. Ensure that there is honesty and truth in both discussions and next steps, versus avoidance and deflection. Can you address the real issue, or does your partner become resentful and blameful when you discuss how you feel? This is not the time to back down; otherwise, you will likely resume previous lines of poor communication and connection. Know and be honest with yourself and what you want, before you move forward from this step.

4. Establish expectations of what you want from your relationship. What is acceptable and what is not? Do you both agree on what is important to each of you and how you should behave? What is not working, and what do you want to change? Both partners will benefit from wanting to improve reactions at times of stress, improve communication to prevent arguments, and determine what is acceptable and the established norms of your relationship. Example: no put-downs, no mocking, acknowledge that both people have a perspective, no arguing in front of children, no hostility, no jealous behavior—whatever is making your relationship toxic.

5. Take time for your relationship and each other; don't take your partner for granted—date nights, romance, outings, exercise together, or anything you like to experience or enjoy together, without friends. Building on experiences that you both enjoy together, and that you can do with each other, is important. Time for intimacy, both emotional and physical, is important so that you both remember that you have a deeper connection to each other over other friendships. Make time to talk, share your day, the morning and night kiss, make each other laugh, make the other person happy with something they like to do—all are

important to maintaining or improving your bond. Find out what you both enjoy doing together.

6. Don't get so caught up in your relationship that you forget who you are. What are your own goals for the future? What do you want to accomplish in life, related to work, family, social time, and even places you want to visit? Essentially, take time for *you,* and nurture who you are and what you want to accomplish in life. Always maintain your own self-confidence, which will help ensure that you get what you deserve, and can prevent/remove yourself from future toxic situations or recurrent toxic relationships.

In my experience with individuals in relationships that are less than ideal, it may take time for anyone to acknowledge that they want more for themselves. Due to the meshing of families and children, it's often not easy to just leave, nor financially feasible. My role at these times is to ensure that people have the resources available to get "out" if they wish. I also recognize that some individuals stay because they have learned to manage their relationship or are waiting for a future date to make a significant change (children to get older, retirement age and pension, etc.).

Each situation is unique, and opinions must be respected. There may be a variety of reasons for someone to choose to stay in a dysfunctional relationship, where partners treat them poorly. Support by close family and friends is necessary to help those manage, as well as time for inner reflection. If there is physical or mental abuse involved, then it is important to make sure those individuals know that others are willing to help and intervene, via numerous resources in the community, as well as possible family or friends.

Part of those resources may involve helping them create a plan to leave. This may mean that they are *still* in the relationship temporarily, but doing the things necessary to prepare financially, mentally, and emotionally to leave.

Setting boundaries before you get into any romantic relationship, is important to help each of you know what the other wants, and define what *you* want from your partner. Enforcing these same expectations is also critical; otherwise, you leave yourself open to your partner taking advantage of your good intentions.

Now that we have discussed toxic relationships in the realm of romance, let's move on to those friendships that enrich our lives yet also have the ability to cause much harm if we are not vigilant about respecting personal boundaries and recognizing our own self-worth. Let's discuss what toxic relationships in friendship looks like, and what you can do to address concerns.

CHAPTER 3
Toxic Friendships

The beauty of healthy friendships is that they can provide a safe means of mutual support and love. These friends help you celebrate any amazing event in your life, grieve with you during times of loss, and create memories with you that add to many wonderful moments in life. The truth is that friendships, outside of romantic relationships, are part of the fabric of who we are as human beings. They ground us, keep us honest, and provide numerous long-term emotional, mental, and physical benefits.

Throughout history, humans have consistently shown a need to be together and interconnect, endeavoring to build bonds with both individuals and within larger communities. We are social beings that thrive when we have continual close interactions with others and can function to our true potential. We have an innate need to be close with others, and can accomplish more when supported by friendships.

What Are Healthy Friendships?

Great friendships enrich our lives, improve our happiness, and reduce stress. They can help you through difficult times, and to better understand why you feel a certain way. Great relationships can act almost as your own personal therapist, to help you through tough times and give you hope at the end. There is an openness that comes with close friends—an honesty that is essential to ensure conversations are real. Good friends help improve your self-confidence, decrease loneliness, increase feelings of self-worth, and encourage personal goal attainment.

Good friendships can be a safe place to air your feelings, allowing you to calm down and come back to family or other relationships with a clearer head and heart. Friends can become a safe sounding board, allowing you to see yourself from different perspectives, looking at both positive and negative positions. Good friendships can help give you a third-party point of view on other relationships in your life, helping provide you insight into another viewpoint when your thoughts are hindered by feelings.

Friendships are not one-size-fits-all. In fact, you might look at your close circle of friends and find that these relationships are different and based on a variety of factors and similarities that you both enjoy—cultural bonds, people whom you have known since childhood, work friends who share workload and stress, those you exercise with, those who you've bonded with over shared experiences or trauma—the list goes on and on. You may also find that some friendships have a more casual component, while other friendships feel closer due to a deeper underlying bond.

While your friendships are going to have their own unique markers that tie you to each other, there are common traits that can be found in all healthy friendships. A healthy friendship is one in which each individual shows care for the other person and has a level of commitment to maintaining the friendship. There is respect for personal space and privacy. Not everyone wants or can be around all friends constantly, but there is still a bond that joins you together. A healthy friendship involves communication, where you can be honest and share your feelings in a respectful way. After all, just because you are friends does not mean that you will always agree with each other. Safe and open communication becomes the key to addressing issues and potential misunderstandings that are bound to happen from time to time. They will also adapt to changing circumstances as you both learn new things and grow.

Recognize that a relationship will change over time. You may consider someone a close friend at one point in your life, but they move away or have changing interests, so you find the relationship changes as a result. It doesn't always mean the relationship ends, but it shifts. Healthy friendships can grow and change without individuals involved feeling as if they are losing out.

Clearly, there are a variety of benefits that you can enjoy as part of a healthy friendship. There is nothing better than the feeling of surrounding yourself with kind, unique, and interesting people who lift you up during the good and bad times. Friendships are not always constant, because some relationships are truly meant to be short-term, as some individuals flow back out of your life. Embrace the time and enrichment you both enjoyed together.

As we age, the benefits of being social become even more important. Studies show that socialization provides many health benefits, including improving cardiovascular health, reducing the risk of disease, boosting your immune system, and the reduction or delay of memory decline— to name just a few. Being happy and having a two-way conversation with a friend is so important to stimulate your mind and keep it healthy. Crosswords and word search puzzles are great, compared to watching TV or an individual activity, but nothing beats the mental and physical benefits of good quality social time with friends.

The benefits of an ever-deepening relationship, the level of intimacy that only comes with long-time friendships, should be part of your plan for a healthy and happy life. But with socialization comes meeting people that are less than desirable and do not add value to you. You may even have current long-term "friends" now that can be difficult to deal with, do not enrich your life, or contribute to your happiness. When a friendship has begun to display toxic elements, you should find yourself wondering if that relationship has reached the end of the line, or if there are steps you can take to repair it. Let's now understand what a toxic relationship may look like.

How Do You Know it is Toxic?

While every friendship goes through its various ups and downs, toxic elements can be introduced to any strong relationship and end up eating away at it. Healthy friendships that end up infested with jealousy or envy easily turn sour or toxic, which can be detrimental to the health of both individuals.

In order to truly understand how a toxic friendship can negatively impact you, it is important to first understand the different types of toxic friendships that take place. This is not an exhaustive list, but you can help evaluate your current relationships considering these points. Do you have any current friendships where you've questioned the amount of effort it takes to maintain them?

Emotional Vampires – These are individuals that prove to be an energy drain, sucking the positivity and peace out of any situation or relationship. They do not just deplete your physical energy but can negatively impact your psychological well-being. After interacting with them, you might find yourself physically tired for an extended and abnormal amount of time. These individuals can make you feel anxious, depressed, and unproductive, causing you to question your own next steps and confidence. They are self-absorbed and manipulative individuals, not always aware of their effects, who drag you down, making you question your own self-worth, ability, and productivity.

> **DEPENDANT** – *She's always upset about something; I just can't take it anymore. Her life is so dysfunctional, and she has so many problems with her family. Honestly, I can hardly believe it's as bad as it is sometimes because there is so much drama. She says her sister told her that she should be lucky to have her loser, cheater husband. Her son has been partying hard and doesn't listen to her. And work, OMG, that's another issue. She says they keep*

bypassing her as a manager, though that doesn't surprise me! She's so hard to deal with sometimes and drives me crazy! I feel so exhausted after we get together.

– Laurel L.

Trust Issues/Privacy/Gossip – The core of any relationship is the ability to trust the other individual with matters that are close to your heart. It is a demonstration of your trust when you share private aspects of your thinking, or the situations you may be dealing with in life. Finding out that your friend has shared these confidences with others, through gossip or malicious talking behind your back, will erode that trust. If you are on the receiving end of this, you will feel hurt, betrayed, and angry. Once trust is lost, it takes significant effort and the willingness of both parties to work towards regaining it.

Unhealthy Competition – Have you had a relationship with an individual who always wants to overshadow every one of your accomplishments with their own? Often, they are so focused on being superior that they don't recognize the effect on your feelings, or how it may be affecting your relationship. Friendly competition is motivating and healthy, helping both of you attain goals—it contributes to a healthy dynamic in your friendship. In comparison, friends that act as rivals, vying to win, or constantly putting you down, are harmful to your self-esteem. True friendships build you up, not tear you down.

Jealousy of Other Friendships – When you have a healthy friendship, you recognize and encourage your friend to have other relationships. This does not negate or lessen the value of your own relationship with that individual. Toxic friendships, on the other hand, have elements of jealousy, where your friend only wants to be with you and tends to discourage you from spending time with others. They may sabotage other friendships by trying to drive wedges into those relationships, pointing out other's faults and becoming angry or annoyed when you see others. Friends that exhibit this type of jealousy may have poor self-confidence, control issues, or a fear of abandonment.

ENVY – *Whenever I plan to get together with friends, it seems that I can't do it without Sally also being included. I want her there most of the time, but some of my friends don't like her as much and would prefer that she not be there all the time. Sometimes people miss out. If I ask her, she says it's fine, but I know she's not happy. She talks about how I've known some friends longer, and maybe I'm closer with them anyway, but it just makes me feel guilty for not inviting her. She has other friends but only seems to want to be with me and whatever I'm doing. It's starting to get tiring!*

– Diane R.

Bad Influence – You may remember your mother telling you that the people you spend time with will contribute to the type of person you will become. When a friendship tends to bring out the worst in you, it may be worth questioning whether it has turned toxic. If your friend is not helping enrich you but is moving you down a path toward a self-destructive lifestyle, or even questionable behavior, then it's moving down a negative path. Another aspect of this type of bad influence is the pressure you feel to not say no, even if your gut or intuition is telling you that the suggestions of your friend are bad ideas. Finding yourself constantly pressured, either internally or externally, means the relationship is moving from a healthy zone and into an unhealthy one.

PRESSURE – *I should be too old to feel peer pressure now, but I still do. Why do I always let myself drink so much when I'm around these same people? I know they aren't going anywhere in life, and they do such stupid things, yet when we get together, it seems so fun. I get caught up in what's happening, then regret my decisions. When I'm not drinking, I'm not happy with their decisions. When I drink, I don't seem to care.*

– Terri C.

Put-Downs/Criticism – Part of any healthy friendship is the need to feel loved and supported. When someone is constantly being put down or censored for their actions, even when there should be no need to do so, that individual doesn't feel encouraged to make decisions for themselves. They don't grow as an individual or feel empowered, and they are less confident with their direction and life decisions. This constant negativity starts to tear down their sense of self-worth and confidence, which again is damaging to their mental and emotional health.

Unequal Relationships/Poor Give and Take – Every relationship has its moments when one friend does more for the other. Healthy relationships have a natural give and take, but it becomes unhealthy or toxic when one person is consistently giving without receiving something in return. An unequal relationship is when one individual has all their needs met or exceeded at the expense of the other individual. There is a draining effect that occurs, much like the emotional vampire. These toxic elements may be affecting your finances, time, emotions, or independence. Ensure that your relationship promotes self-independence and self-reliance and that you don't overburden your friendships. You need to feel confident in yourself before you can truly be a good friend to someone else.

> **SELFISH** – *We're friends, mostly. I mean, our families have all done dinner together several times. Our girls are in the same grade and are close. I feel sorry for the daughter since her mother is never willing to pick her up from school or bring her over to her friends' houses— even when she's home. Her daughter is now at our place all the time. I can't tell you how many dinners I've fed her, and her parents never seem to care how much she's away. They don't reciprocate with my daughter, and I'm getting a little fed up with it now. I also think it's affecting my daughter's grades. This girl is always here, and they don't always focus on homework. I also end up having to drive her home in the evening!*
>
> *– Angela V.*

Excessive Drama – There is always that one individual we know who seems to contribute to an excessive amount of turmoil in almost any situation. And let's be honest, it can be exhausting! These friends can turn the focus onto themselves no matter what is happening, no matter where you are. They have an innate need to be the center of attention, even if the focus for an event should be for someone else. They are the friend that causes drama when you go out, blowing situations out of proportion and forcing you into a position to support or rescue them—even if you don't agree with what they've said. Their over-exaggeration or overly emotional reactions to situations cause stress in friend groups.

Crossing Boundaries – All of us have boundaries, ones that we put up for personal protection or to maintain our personal space and privacy. When those boundaries are crossed, they make us feel uncomfortable and angry or annoyed. While the opinions from other friends may be well-intentioned, at times even requested, other occasions may be considered intrusive and crossing the line of friendship. No one should tell someone else what to do, and nobody really knows what's in a relationship—so be respectful that certain opinions should be censored or omitted.

> **INTRUSION** – *Look, I know they are trying to help, but I'm not looking for their opinion. I know they don't think it's a good idea for us to live with my mother, but it's fine. She's a widow now, and it's not going to affect my marriage. She needs our help. Yes, everyone needs to be flexible a bit and work together, but I know it will work out. My wife and mother will be fine together, and frankly, my friends who keep talking to my wife negatively about it need to butt out. It's not their business.*
>
> *– Frank M.*

Often, toxic friendships end up having several interwoven elements that overlap each other. How these toxic relationships negatively affect your health, personal life, emotional wellbeing, and confidence may not be as obvious. As you reflect on your current friendships, you may be realizing that you do have some that fall into these categories. Some relationships might feel manageable, others less so—it depends on what experiences you've already shared, and how close you really feel to this person. Before you decide whether to maintain or end a friendship with toxic elements, it is important to understand what the impact of these relationships can have on you over time.

The Risks of Toxic Friendships

While healthy friendships can bring us plenty of benefits, both emotionally and physically, toxic relationships can bring negative consequences, both short and long-term. Here are just a few things to consider while evaluating some of your more challenging friendships.

Depression – When you have friendships where you are constantly being drained emotionally, and torn down through criticism and put-downs, the impact can negatively undermine your sense of self-worth. Many individuals find themselves slipping into a depression or dealing with other emotional issues. As the relationship progresses, it is likely that the negative emotional impact will only grow and flow to other aspects of your life. Work, your partner, children, other friendships—unhappiness and despair from one relationship will cloud how you interact with other bonds as well.

Physical Decline – There is a deep connection between our mental health and our physical well-being. For those dealing with depression or other emotional issues, the struggle is likely to manifest into physical issues. Toxic friendships can feed into that decline, because how you feel, impacts your actions and health—these manifest with different effects like poor sleeping habits, not eating, eating the wrong foods, emotional drinking, or skipping exercise. When feeling sad, overburdened, or frustrated, most people will start to ignore healthier options to deal with stress. While we'd all love to be those people who exercise more when stressed, that's sadly not the reality for most people—self-neglect is more common.

Poor Self-Esteem – Our self-concept is tied to our sense of self-worth. Having a friend that is constantly tearing you down through criticism, neglect, or a continual need for attention, is draining you of your emotional resources. The friendship is no longer uplifting or supportive, as it continues to drain you and makes you start to doubt your own worth. Your idea of self is constructed by the beliefs you hold about yourself, as well as responses from others in your life. If reactions from your friends are primarily negative, then it poorly impacts your self-concept, making you doubt yourself and your abilities.

Isolation from Other Relationships – One of the many beauties in life can be found in the relationships we create. The diversity in bonds with many people, both new or old, and different from us, contributes to making us better, more well-rounded people. Toxic friendships can make us retreat from others due to the challenges that come with jealousy or feelings of poor self-worth. We start doubting what we contribute to other relationships, and pull away, deepening feelings of depression and poor self-esteem. The draining impact of these friendships can lead to further isolation and the loss of healthy friendships, leaving you only with the toxic friendships that continue to devour you.

Clearly, a reoccurring theme is the many risks to your emotional, physical, and mental well-being when you have toxic friendships in your life. Any friendship can start healthy but turn into something unhealthy due to any number of factors in your own or the other person's personality. Do you see any toxic aspects in any of your current relationships, and can you save them? On the other hand, you may now feel that a relationship is too toxic and not worth saving; perhaps it's soured to the point where they are no longer worth the effort. How can you make the best decisions for this relationship? Plus, what steps can you take to deal with a toxic friendship?

Finding Solutions for Toxic Friendships

1. One of the first things I want you to do is to write down all the pros and cons of this relationship. How do you interact with each other? Can you think of several ways that both of you contribute positively to the relationship? What are either of you doing that negatively impacts the relationship

or the other person? Once you start making your list, reflect on it for a few days. You might be surprised at what comes to you after taking some time to think about these points, focusing on how that relationship makes you feel, and what you may be doing to add to the toxicity. Remember, in toxic relationships, it is never only one person's fault. If you are allowing someone to treat you poorly, write this down as one of your contributing attributes. Use points from earlier in the chapter to help you understand the various aspects of your list, and whether they would fall under the healthy or unhealthy relationship status.

2. Next, I want you to take that list and focus on a few key points. Often, the larger part of the list is not just the surface symptoms, but the true reason that your relationship has turned toxic is much deeper. Take the time to mentally dig down and identify if this relationship has previously had negative aspects, and when they started. What do you anticipate this friend will say about your relationship and its negative attributes? Consider your responses and their possible points of view.

3. Plan to sit down and talk with your friend. Calmly express how you feel, doing so without judgment and anger—remember, you are trying to repair this relationship. Your impulse may be to attack them for what you now identify as inappropriate behaviors in your friendship, but you cannot start any progress if you sabotage initial discussions.

4. Do not focus on just expressing yourself, but allow your friend to talk as well. You may find that you both have concerns that can be addressed together. Solutions may result from your conversation as you both contribute thoughts and feelings. However, if the situation turns ugly, or the conversation becomes attacking in nature, it may be best to walk away for a time. The point of this talk is about making your relationship better, not starting a heated

argument that ends with feeling worse off and with no solutions.

If things do get heated, give some time for cooling off, and then try to come together again—if you are both in agreement. Focus on finding a mutually acceptable agreement, one that leaves both of you excited to work on building up your friendship. Granted, you may find that not every relationship is going to move forward with both parties excited about fixing these issues. In fact, you might find the relationship ending, simply because you both can't come together with a resolution.

5. Regardless of how the discussion ends, you now need to take time for yourself—this is time for self-love. What have you been missing out on while spending so much time doing things with someone that made you unhappy? Throughout this process, start creating boundaries important to you in your friendships. What do you want out of a friendship? Learn how to recognize when it crosses a line and becomes unhealthy; then take steps to care for yourself. Understand that change is an ongoing part of any friendship. Focus on providing to others the same things you want for yourself.

In the meantime, while you are working on repairing a toxic friendship, take the time to maintain your other relationships. Be a healthy friend, and contribute to your interactions with others in a meaningful way. This will help draw like-minded friends to you, giving you the chance to create new friendships. You will likely find that older relationships grow more meaningful as you grow as a person and share your newfound insight.

No matter what type of friend you have, remember that no relationship remains static over time. If you see a friendship beginning to turn toxic, talk with them early, before things get out of hand, and try to repair the relationship to move it back onto a healthy footing. Recognize that there will, over time, be people you end your relationship with, as people change or grow apart. If things do turn negative, be willing to love yourself enough to walk away if it's not possible to repair the relationship or positively address the toxic elements.

The fact is that platonic friendships have an important place in all our lives. Nurturing them is key to having a full and joyful life. However, if your relationships have toxic elements, they can have negative risks and health effects. Evaluate your friendships, and make sure they are still healthy for both of you. I am currently developing an exciting and interactive program to guide you toward setting and implementing your personal change goals. If you feel you want more in life, this step-by-step program will be for you! Visit **jillhartzog.com** for more information.

CHAPTER 4
Toxic Relationships at Work

When it comes to our work and careers, all of us recognize that there will be numerous relationships and interactions with co-workers and clients that will be challenging and less than healthy. Due to the nature of your job or work guidelines, you may feel cornered and limited in your responses, compared to how you would handle similar situations in other areas of your life. It is unlikely that you can just walk away or cut off ties, as you could with other situations and people.

There are numerous types of toxic relationships that frequently occur at work, but when is it too much, and how can you manage them? It's not healthy or acceptable to just ignore people that abuse you, regardless if it's at work or not, so something must change. Let's discuss the benefits of healthy relationships and safe work environments to help us better identify those that are toxic or destructive to our health.

The Benefits of a Healthy and Safe Workplace

For most of us, the workplace is where we spend the largest part of our day. If you work full time, you will spend much more time with the people you work with than with your family and friends. Keeping this in mind, the better the work environment, the healthier it is for our own wellness and those we love. The social impact of our work atmosphere trickles down to our mental, physical, and emotional health—and subsequently affects our relationships with family and friends.

Employers benefit from promoting a healthy and safe work environment in several important ways, the most important to them being productivity. If you have ever worked in a friendly and supportive environment, you know this to be true. The positivity of the climate motivates everyone and improves performance levels. Motivated employees increase their productivity and energy simply by not being distracted by troubled relationships or interactions with others—the positive environment suppresses those issues. The employee (you), in turn, feels invested in the company when there is a sense of team or family, when you like who you work with or for. The added benefit is that there is no sense of dread or anxiety when you wake up and get ready for work each day.

When you are dealing with a less than ideal work environment, you feel high stress, which negatively impacts your physical and mental well-being. *Have you noticed a trend yet, how negative stress affects your body?* This stress may leave you feeling drained, depressed, or angry, and neither is beneficial for your long-term health. How many of us have ever taken a day off from work, referring to it as a *mental health day?* Too often, it occurs and relates back to the level of stress that we are feeling at our place of employment.

Dealing with stress can manifest physically in terms of frequent headaches, neck and back pain, frequent colds, weight gain, constant fatigue, and insomnia, as well as mentally in terms of difficulty making decisions, increased frustration, excessive defensiveness, problems communicating, difficulty concentrating, forgetfulness, and trouble learning.

Clearly, you can see how negativity impacts your performance at work and your ability to be productive. For businesses, the impact of that stress translates into more missed days, lower overall efficiency, higher turnover of employees, increased workers' compensation, and higher medical insurance expenses.

When a company's work environment becomes toxic, it can become quite challenging to acquire new talent. Current and former employees can spread negative information to the public, which degrades potential future employees' interest. Constant staff turnover costs money in lost productivity, advertising, and training new staff, not to mention the additional stress and workload placed on current employees covering open positions. There is an additional toll of lost skills and experience, which can be invaluable to a growing company.

Healthy and safe work environments are the key to reducing stress on the job and its unhealthy impact on employees. When you have a safe and functional workplace, people are happy and perform better, with each other and towards clients. Staff will stay where they feel appreciated and valued. Loyalty to the company increases, with fewer staff turnovers and decreased associated costs—which is clearly a win-win for everyone.

If you are a business owner looking to shift your company's unhealthy culture, we will be covering some valuable ways to reduce stress and create a healthier environment for your employees. If you are a frustrated employee, we will explore frequent toxic issues at work, and steps you can take to improve the environment, decreasing the stress levels of everyone on the team.

If you are re-entering the workforce, then you are facing the challenges of those missing years of experience or skills. Fellow co-workers might be quick to get frustrated, and may even attempt to sabotage your efforts to integrate. You may face the systematic prejudice that may result because you are now older and have renewed pursuing your career.

The public, or customers, can also bring a level of toxicity into your job as well. For example, customers who are frustrated with the company may direct their animosity to whichever employee is at hand, which might be you. Any of us who works in a customer service industry, directly with the public, has likely at some point been on the receiving end of verbal abuse. The result is that you are placed in a position where you must measure your response and reaction, even when you want to snap something back. At work, we all must learn how to deal effectively and professionally with negative situations from all possible people we are required to work with.

Types of Toxic Behavior in the Workplace

People have such interesting and complex personalities, coming from so many different backgrounds, with vastly diverse upbringings and values. To find and fall in love with another person in life is such an interesting phenomenon. Two strangers need to find each other, someone they get along well with, to live and love together. This is the development of any relationship, over which you have much control. Now instead, force together an entire room or building full of strangers who don't have the same level of similarity, yet must spend most of their waking hours together. What do you think you get? Some possibly quite explosive relationship dynamics. There is a reason people refer to their work-family or work-spouse—you can be with these people, on average, one-third of all the hours in your life.

We don't have to be friends with our boss, employee, or coworker; we don't even have to like them—we just need to be able to deal with them well enough that we can work effectually together. You need to be able to complete the tasks and projects required, but unfortunately, this is not always possible. When work relationships deteriorate, it can significantly impact the workplace, trickling down to affect other employees and the reputation of the workplace itself. What many people term as *office politics*, often refers to the dysfunctional culture within a company; and people are aware but are unwilling or unable to affect change. What are some of the more common toxic relationships people experience at work?

Bullying and harassment are two of the most prominent behaviors found in toxic work environments. Often, those exhibiting these behaviors are focused on undermining and intimidating potential rivals. They may be focused on preventing this person from being promoted or looking to make themselves look better by belittling someone else. Talking behind someone's back, making demeaning comments, misusing power through humiliation, or preventing them from gaining the status they deserve, are all forms of harassment.

> **HARASS** – *When I get home from work, I am so stressed for the first hour, feeling that the phone is going to ring from the unit. There are three ladies there that bully everyone, but since I push back a bit, they are always looking for things I did wrong. They follow my shift and are always critical of what I did during the day. When I work a double shift, they make sure I have the hardest assignment, and they don't offer any help. They always talk behind my back. The looks they give me are so inappropriate, but what can I do? My manager isn't a strong leader.*
>
> *– Polly A.*

Being bullied is a deliberate action and one that has the intention to invoke harm on their victim. Those who are bullied and harassed have increased stress, diminished confidence and, eventually, degraded work performance.

Harassment can occur through many routes at work, including sexual harassment, which leaves individuals feeling unsafe in the workplace, and disrespected as an equal employee. Verbal innuendos, inappropriate comments, physical touching, or offering work benefits for sexual favors, are all signs of sexual harassment. Victims may feel they have little recourse if this is occurring from a person of authority, over a concern that their career could be in jeopardy. When conditions worsen, and there is no obvious or easy solution, many will resort to quitting their job, which will cause further emotional stress and add financial difficulties to the victim.

There are numerous other forms of toxic work relationships that could occur between colleagues, managers, and employees, and even from your customers themselves. Some behaviors that are exhibited towards others at work, make the environment difficult; others can make it nearly intolerable. These may include the following destructive actions:

Micromanagement of your job when it's not required. Your boss or coworker is constantly monitoring what you are doing, so you don't have the freedom to make your own decisions.

> **HANDLE** – *It's near impossible to make any decisions at work anymore! The managers have taken away our ability to make almost any autonomous decisions for ourselves—we have to ask for permission to do everything. I have been a professional in this industry for over 25 years, yet they constantly want to micromanage me! Now I must send an email to my manager for the smallest thing, beginning with what's required for safety, then wait for another 2–3 days till I hear back. It's ridiculous and frustrating for everyone!*
>
> *–Tina Y.*

Taking credit for your work or ideas, and making it their own.

Not taking responsibility for their own poor decisions or when missed deadlines occur due to their own poor work performance or organization skills.

Non-conformist is the person always undermining workplace policy and pushing their own agenda or way of doing things. While risk takers can be good in some positions of a company, overall it can be very detrimental to employee morale, causing confusion and holding back the performance of the team.

One-person-show tends to be the employee who acts like a know-it-all, who undermines group productively and creativity. This person loves to talk and take over conversations, again pushing their own agenda or is unwilling to act as a team player.

Overly critical of work assignments. They do not accept that it is their responsibility or position to perform the assigned tasks. Conversely, when assignments are completed, a manager is unaccepting or unappreciative of a job well done.

Unrealistic deadlines that are given to staff, or demanded by customers, that are inappropriate, risk safety, and create chaos and high stress.

The kindergarten mentality occurs when all employees are punished or reprimanded equally, instead of their manager dealing appropriately with an individual employee. This is taking the easy way out, and it undermines good employees who are good performers, causing mass frustration and anger in the workplace. I can't stress this enough since I've experienced it myself many times over the years.

> **PRESCHOOL** – *Seriously, I can't believe they want to schedule our entire day. If there are some people who can't do the job, why can't they discipline them? Instead, everyone gets punished, just because management is unable to address issues with those that can't do their job! I feel like I'm back in kindergarten again!*
>
> *– Laura T.*

Drama creators are those who constantly create problems at work or bring their own family drama to work, which adversely affects others.

Demands outside work hours occur too often in some industries and it can be hard to draw a line for non-unionized positions, since work hours in a day or week may be less well-defined. Employees must be able to draw a line between work and family time, to prevent long-term stress and inevitable health decline.

Constant negativity is the way a person communicates with others or handles projects and work assignments. These people will often complain without having their own solution to the problem at hand, and take more time complaining than just getting the job done.

> **ADVERSE** – *While I'm frustrated with the new project also, I know there isn't much that can be done to stop it, and (sigh) I'm just going to make the best of it. But this one guy I work with just can't*

stop complaining about every little thing, and it wastes so much time! He is always negative and constantly complains about every part he's assigned to do. If he would just do his job, we'd all be done quicker.

– Mike G.

Unfair workloads between staff or peers, or special treatment towards employees who are friends with management.

Manipulation of others and events that occur in the workplace. Going behind the backs of other employees to get in good standing with the boss. Lying or exaggerating with malicious and deliberate intent.

GROVEL – *I walked into our meeting today, my job performance review. Can you believe that my manager still had an email open from one of my colleagues that talked about me?! She closed it after I walked in, but not before I saw it, where she was saying that I would not cover one of her workdays—and they were talking back and forth about me! So inappropriate, but what can I do? All she wants to do is suck up to our manager.*

– Johanna S.

Procrastinators and lazy employees who hold everyone up and can't focus on assigned tasks.

Excessive social time at work occurs when an employee views their job as an extension of their social time, instead of performing their job. Excessive breaks, social calls, or time on social media cause disruption to other employees and workload, possibly encouraging the same behavior in others.

Passive-aggressive individuals may appear to go along with company decisions but then subtly work against them, undermining other's accomplishments or workplace decisions. Passive-aggressive tendencies are surprisingly quite destructive to the work environment and other co-workers. Here are a few of the ways that passive-aggressiveness can show up in the workplace.

Toxic Relationships at Work

- Using sick days during crunch periods or major projects, thus disrupting the productivity of the group—often "disappearing" during those critical points, forcing workloads to be readjusted.

- Spreading malicious rumors about co-workers, management, or the company they work for.

- They refuse to go the extra mile for the team, often using the phrase "that's not my job." Time after time, extra work falls onto other people while they minimize their own workload.

- Resisting feedback focused on self-improvement.

- 'Forgetting' to complete tasks or complete assignments by deadlines.

- Redirecting conversations to the actions of others to deflect attention.

- Using email to avoid face-to-face communication with other individuals on the team; communicating complaints via email or text, to avoid face-to-face confrontations.

All these actions may be aimed at avoiding responsibility for specific tasks. They could be suppressing anger regarding promotions or an intense dislike of individuals in the office. Their actions may be focused on making some individuals look bad, often by withholding information, doing less than they were supposed to, missing deadlines, and making excuses when things are not completed.

Constantly dealing with negative situations at work takes a large toll on your mental and physical health. Trouble sleeping, depression, and bringing stress home affects your own health as well as those in your family. Work toxicity negatively impacts ongoing job performance and the ability to move up professionally, so how can we work around or through these issues?

Too often, when work boundaries and accepted norms are violated, the victims in these situations struggle to know what to do or how to feel safe. If you are dealing with any of these toxic elements, it can be a challenge to get up and go to work each day. Long-term mental stress leads to physical decline like high blood pressure, weight gain, diabetes—no different from any of the effects caused by other stress-related relationships discussed in previous chapters. How can you or your employer address these issues in order to care for your own well-being, and improve your workplace environment?

Improving Workplace Relationships Despite Toxic Elements

One of the first things to remember is that you can always choose how you will react to others, regardless of how they act toward you. While they might be behaving inappropriately, your actions can mitigate the impact of those actions on the situation you're dealing with and company culture at large. That being said—and I want to be clear—there are some toxic environments that cannot be ignored or handled by you alone. In these situations, obtaining the help of others will be required, such as elevating incidents to your manager, director, or human resources department.

If elements become too great to overcome, and you are not receiving the support you require, or these incidents involve those that run the company and oversee your career, you may need to consider finding different employment. With that in mind, there are several options to first consider when reviewing your choices and the severity of your workplace environment—before making the leap to finding new employment.

1. Assess the situation: What is *actually* happening to make you feel uncomfortable or upset at work? At times, this is obvious if you are dealing with one person. Other times, there is an underlying level of animosity or distrust in the

workplace, one that has persisted for years. What do you think the specific issue is?

2. If you identify a specific individual that is causing you difficulties, are you able to distance yourself from them? That might involve minimizing how much time you spend together in the course of performing your job, or altering your breaks to avoid contact with them outside of necessary work interactions. While not every job will give you this option, it can often be a way of minimizing the impacts of dealing with these individuals.

3. Align yourself with other coworkers who provide better support and could be experiencing similar difficulties at work. This may be helpful as you work towards a better work environment and present a united front for future actions.

4. If you are experiencing harassment at work, does your company have human resource policies on employee expectations and conduct? Be aware, you may want to refer to this as you bring complaints forward.

5. Start documenting all incidents that are inappropriate at work. This will be required if you file a formal complaint. Save emails and text messages; write down comments from meetings, and any inappropriate incidents that occur at work.

6. Talk with your direct supervisor if appropriate, any other supervisor, or your human resource department. Is it possible that they are unaware of what has been occurring— bringing it up to other's attention is key. Administrators have a legal obligation to address issues, but if they are not willing to do so, you may need to seek legal advice.

7. Does your company offer any type of mediation? You may consider using this avenue to discuss boundaries and work

relationships. Having the ability to discuss your situation can be key to addressing toxic elements in ways that benefit all parties. Was the other party unaware of how they were acting? Are they willing to work on their conduct? Do they agree to work on their behavior, during mediation, yet then act contrary to what was agreed upon?

If the level of toxicity is beyond mediation, this would be when formal action against another coworker would occur, and they may be put on a disciplinary action plan or fired for their conduct. Having documentation to support your claims will be extremely important to support this level of intervention.

8. Start your exit strategy, and plan what you need to do if you need to leave this work environment. If you already suspect that things are not likely to change, remember to consider your own long-term health if choosing to remain in a toxic work atmosphere. Pay off bills and start shifting more money into savings. Do your best to find another job before you leave, so that you do not have the additional stress of financial difficulties. Searching for new employment does not have to be the last step; this can be done during any of the steps above.

9. If you feel that your issues are a human rights complaint, and your work environment is not adequately addressing your harassment, then consider seeking legal advice in your local district, or adequate compensation if you have lost your job.

Throughout the entire time you are working on this problem, do your best to maintain your positivity when dealing with other co-workers. Again, depending on what level of toxicity you're dealing with, you might be surprised at how general positivity can improve a relationship, or at least maintain other workplace relationships. Once you start the process of addressing a toxic work situation, you may find that your workplace reputation takes a hit—so having some supportive co-workers will help during this time.

Assessing the risks to your professional reputation will help you decide if you should move forward with a formal complaint or just plan to leave the environment. While bringing forth complaints is your legitimate right when addressing inappropriate actions at work, you are likely to receive some pushback, especially from those who you are making the complaint against, or those unhappy with any change. If the toxic relationship is with a manager, you may find yourself dealing with worse work tasks, poor reviews, and other methods of retaliation from your complaint.

Certain behaviors need to be brought to light in order to correct corporate culture. While the results of your complaint might mean that you have to deal with some pushback, or still result in a choice to move on, you may be the catalyst that allows others to be relieved of dealing with that toxic relationship. Map out your plans for what you are willing to accept.

Escaping toxic relationships in the workplace can be complicated, but once you make the decision that you deserve better, you won't be able to settle for less. Going through this process will help you handle future work relationships and possible dysfunction. No matter what you decide regarding how to deal with toxic workplace relationships, never forget the importance of self-care. Take time to de-stress after work, and mentally put distance between the workplace and your home life. Work out, be with friends and family; distract yourself from what you're dealing with at work.

From time to time, there will be jobs that you can't (initially) afford to leave, even with the varying levels of toxic relationships you encounter. Spending more time caring for yourself, and focusing on maintaining your own physical and mental health, will better see you through times of high stress and poor work conditions until you can eventually move to another location, position, or job.

CHAPTER 5

Toxic Relationship with Your Mental Health

Throughout this journey of toxic relationships, I have discussed different aspects of your life where a toxic relationship can raise its head and create great dysfunction. There are always options available to handle a deteriorating relationship, including making the decision to fix or end an association. However, there is one relationship that you cannot simply walk away from, or even easily fix—how you view and perceive yourself.

Our mental health and ability to cope with the difficulties life throws at us is very individual to each of us. As situations arise, we all react differently as determined by our individual life experiences and our learned ability to cope. What some consider a toxic or nonfunctioning relationship, others may easily ignore, or simply dismiss the situation as significant. The stronger our emotional health, the more resilient and able to cope we become when dealing with difficult situations that arise. Let's all agree that life is full of interesting, challenging, and difficult situations—but it's how we cope with them that sets us up for success or failure.

Maintaining optimal emotional and mental health will make life appear much less difficult, and more enjoyable overall. Quality of life, both actual and perceived, is key. Maintaining our mental health, for long-term stability, is important through the different stages of our growth and advancing age as family, friends, work, health, and relationships change.

There are many signs you need to be aware of that indicate you are not maintaining optimal mental health. Lacking feelings of joy, happiness, desire, or motivation, and not maintaining relationships with others, are all clear indicators of declining quality of life. Let's reinforce the benefits of well-balanced mental health, identify when it's not occurring, and then help you regain or maintain mental stability.

The Benefits of Stable Mental Health

Good mental health has often been characterized by our ability to fulfill a variety of functions and activities, such as the ability to learn, to express oneself, and to be able to manage a full range of emotions (both good and bad). The ability to form lasting relationships with others, and the ability to manage and cope with change, also illustrates balanced mental health.

One of the ways to evaluate your mental health is by looking at how well you can accomplish your goals. Many individuals who struggle with mental health matters find it challenging to set and meet various goals in their personal and professional lives. Your goals are part of the learning and growth that we all experience throughout our lives. When you have quality mental health, you can recognize areas or habits that you should change or learn from. As a result, you can set goals and then create a plan to achieve them.

Various life experiences contribute to your mental health as well. If you've had more positive experiences and opportunities in life, outweighing the bad, then you are more likely to learn and build a cache of wisdom and coping mechanisms. Alternatively, those who have had to live with constant negativity and adversity have much more to overcome and must direct more effort into acquiring their own survival skills.

Toxic Relationship with Your Mental Health

We all learn from the many different experiences we're exposed to in life, and we all grow as a result of them. Perhaps you were able to make changes that positively impacted your life. Experiencing failure or defeat does not mean that you, yourself, are a failure, and having optimal mental health helps you to understand the difference in this regard.

When your mental health is good, you are better able to maintain your physical health, simply because you can make the connection between your physical and mental wellbeing. Those who struggle with various mental health concerns cannot always focus on the attention needed to care for themselves physically. Mental and physical health are symbiotic of each other, causing suffering if either one is neglected or out of balance for too long. In the next chapter, we will further discuss our relationship with our own physical health, but for now, let's discuss how important it is to maintain our mental well-being.

Throughout this book, I have focused on a variety of toxic relationships and how they impact you or others. One of the ways that decides how much you are impacted in any situation is the stability of your mental health. Think about how positive relationships in your life can serve to uplift you and help you to grow, feel supported, and motivate you to reach out to others. Quality relationships are a two-way street and give you a mental boost. When your mental health is good, you make better relationship choices of who you wish to associate with, which will positively impact your life.

Another aspect of good mental health is its positive impact on your ability to choose and reach professional goals. We all know that achieving school or work goals typically translates into a higher income throughout your lifetime. Every goal you meet provides more opportunities that come your way. When you feel motivated to go after these opportunities, you feel positive about yourself and your accomplishments.

Throughout this discussion, we focus on how *good* mental health can positively impact your life. These effects provide reciprocal positive feedback that continues to improve your mental resilience over time.

Coping mechanics are copied and seen by others in your life, allowing you to be a positive role model for those around you. By exhibiting stable mental health traits as you navigate obstacles and challenges, you are then demonstrating an appropriate example of healthy coping for your children and others to copy. They can then incorporate these strategies into their own lives so that they too can enjoy the benefits of good health. Happiness is addictive, but misery loves company—which do you want to promote?

There are also signs you can identify that show declining mental health in yourself or those around you. Learn how to identify dysfunction, and what options are available to get well.

Understanding Declined Mental Health

There are many possibilities for why people experience declining mental health, and the medical field is full of numerous articles and studies discussing the hows and whys of various mental health conditions and dysfunction. To add to this complexity, there is no exact and same treatment for all individuals or conditions—what works for one person may not work for the next. The personality of an individual; their underlying body chemistry, composition, and metabolism; their coping ability and how they react to stress—any number of these factors, and more, can contribute to why a person is diagnosed with a medical condition, and what treatment may be needed.

Significant Mental Health Issues

It can be obvious in some cases that someone has declined mental health, such as a mechanical brain injury, compared to the less obvious, like undiagnosed disease progression. Significant mental health issues are harder to treat and take a multitude of supports, from family and friends to counseling and a variety of doctors, depending on the diagnosis. Also, depending on what is occurring in your life, how you're able to cope, and what is happening in your body or to your emotions, there are numerous reasons for experiencing significant cognitive decline. Additionally, not everyone with the same diagnosis will have the same or any mental health deterioration at all (e.g., depression or anxiety), so this list is very subjective.

Influencing Physical Factors

- Head injury (trauma)
- Imbalanced brain chemicals (e.g., serotonin and dopamine changes)
- Neurological conditions that cause brain changes (e.g., epilepsy, multiple sclerosis, dementia, Parkinson's)
- Family history (poor learned coping skills, genetics)
- Drug and alcohol addiction (significant, poor coping)

Influencing Societal/Emotional Factors

- Long-term stress (e.g., various types of abuse and trauma)
- High sudden stress episodes (e.g., the death of a loved one; loss of a job and financial instability; poor coping with a new health condition; physical health decline, where it is prolonged and the person is not coping)

Remember, what causes one person to experience significant mental health decline and an inability to function may not be the same for someone else. Additionally, while one person cannot easily manage past a societal or emotional crisis, another person may be able to cope much easier, with additional support, counseling, or medical intervention.

Milder Mental Health Issues

The focus of this chapter is really to discuss milder forms of mental health dysfunction and possible ways to help yourself or loved ones. Significant mental health issues, both societal and physical, require professional management and monitoring beyond what can be accomplished at home. Seek out the appropriate level of support needed for yourself or your loved one.

There is any number of milder reasons any one of us can suddenly or gradually have poor coping abilities with mental health decline. You may think that it won't happen to you, but there are many events that can impact our lives and test our ability to manage stress. Don't judge others—you never know what may test *you* one day.

Possible contributors to milder mental health dysfunctions are:

- Family history (poor learned coping skills, genetics)

- Drug and alcohol abuse (an individual is still moderate/high functioning)

- High sudden stress episodes, short-term in length – this will also depend on an individual's perspective on this (e.g., shorter-term abuse or trauma, postpartum depression, loss of a job, death of a loved one, coping with health issues, coping with society or family stressors and so much more)

Notice that there is an overlap between these lists, where one situation can be extremely damaging and long-term to one person, while another individual can start to manage with time and support from family and friends. All of us can experience any number of events that put us just that little bit over, causing you to feel just a bit sadder or angrier with a situation that at another time you may have accepted. Identifying when you can no longer manage is key to reaching out for the intervention and help you need, before you cannot fully cope with a difficult incident. Make stable mental health your priority to be able to enjoy life to the fullest and be the best you possible!

Signs of Declining Mental Health

Depression

This effect on your mental health can be triggered for a variety of different reasons, and its impact can be significant. According to the American Psychiatric Association, "Depression is a medical illness that affects how you feel, the way you think, and how you act. It may cause feelings of sadness, feelings of pain, as well as a loss of interest in activities that you may have once enjoyed."[2]

Depression is not the occasional bad day where you feel sad or frustrated with issues that arise. It is an overwhelming and persistent feeling of bleakness for which you cannot interrupt these emotions on your own. Your mood is affected and can range at different times from high to low, with feelings that can include emptiness, despondence, agitation, and being easily annoyed over small issues.

One of the realities of depression is that it can contribute to feelings of worthlessness or guilt, difficulty in thinking, concentrating, and decision making, as well as physical symptoms, such as a loss of energy, increased fatigue, inability to sleep at night, changes in appetite, and weight loss or gain. In severe cases, there may even be thoughts of suicide, often related to perceptions of feeling empty or worthless.

> **UNHAPPY** – *I'm not sure why I'm gaining so much weight; it's not like I eat a lot during the day. You'd think all the stress I have to deal with, between my kids and my parents, would make me skinny as a rail. There is never any time for me and what I want to do anymore. That course I signed up for, it's not getting done. I'm always being pulled away, which makes me feel worse since it cost so much. My brain feels so foggy anyway; I don't think I can focus. I'm always wide awake at 3 am and then tired all day.*
>
> *– Sonia W.*

---

[2] https://www.psychiatry.org/patients-families/depression/what-is-depression

It is estimated that depression affects one in 15 adults in any given year. Some individuals may deal with ongoing bouts of depression for months or years; others will always have to work on how they feel, always struggling to handle various tasks necessary in life. While depression can strike anyone at any age, often, it has been noted to start during the late teens and early twenties, with women more likely to suffer than men.

Anxiety

For those dealing with anxiety, it is the combination of the mind and body reacting to stressful, dangerous, or unfamiliar situations. While a certain level of anxiety is healthy because it keeps us alert and aware, the reality is that those suffering from high levels of anxiety can be left completely debilitated. Anxiety disorders may keep you from sleeping, concentrating, interacting with others, or even leaving your home.

Anxiety can reach a level where it needs to be treated, especially if it ends up being irrational, disproportionate to the situation, and overwhelming to the point that it impedes your ability to function in everyday life. Sufferers can feel as if they have no control, with overwhelming feelings of fear and worry, while also dealing with physical symptoms, such as headaches, nausea, or trembling.

> **ANXIOUS** – *When I find myself in a large crowd of people, I feel irritable. If I can't get away, I feel stressed and annoyed; it feels intolerable to me. My wife gets frustrated, but it feels overwhelming, and I just can't deal with it. I avoid busy malls, crowded movie theatres, and anyplace where there are too many people.*
>
> *– Frank T.*

There are multiple types of anxiety disorders related to trauma and stress or tied to obsessive-compulsive disorders. Anxiety can also be tied to a specific phobia, which is related to excessive fear of a specific object or situation. Think of those expressing fear of heights, various animals, social interactions, or the sight of blood. The fear can be related to anything, something a person has had previous experience with or instead has worry and anticipation towards. Any of these situations can contribute to high levels of anxiety, but manifest excessively in a person with an anxiety disorder.

Individuals are frequently diagnosed with both depression and anxiety, as one disorder commonly feeds into the other. People often worry about their feelings of depression and what they can't do or how it's affecting others. Those that experience anxiety and worry over situations or objects, in turn, feel sad and depressed regarding the situation. While depression and anxiety are two separate diagnoses, more than half of people diagnosed with either illness experience both at the same time,[3] making treatment even more challenging.

Poor Self-Care or Self-Sabotage

If you are unable to recognize your value, then it can be easy to believe that you don't deserve self-care. You may also simply forget or feel you have no energy to care for yourself. This lack of attention may also show up in forms of self-sabotage where your actions or behaviors are counter-intuitive and end up harming your physical health, your ability to function at work, or your inter-personal relationships.

> **DESTRUCTIVE** – *I'm fine; I don't care what I look like. Who's coming to see me anyway? You don't count; you're not helping me anyway, so why should I listen to you? No, I don't need a shower; I'm fine the way I am.*
>
> *– Tom H.*

Tom presented with long, dirty hair and grimy bare feet; he had not showered for months, and never brushed his teeth. It is not uncommon for people in this frame of mind to have poor insight into their physical

---

3 Anxiety and Depression Association of America. https://adaa.org/about-adaa/press-room/facts-statistics

decline, and to be reluctant to accept help from others. This would be an advanced example of poor self-care.

Over time, a lack of self-care can result in further health declines, such as a worn-down immune system, significant weight change, or poor effects from a lack of basic grooming—infections, hair loss, or skin breakdown, to name a few. Think of all the ways that you care for yourself on a daily basis; then imagine eliminating them one-by-one. Without treatment for this underlying condition, over time you would continue to feel more despondent and worn out—physically, mentally, and emotionally—continuing in a downward spiral of self-neglect.

Emotional Withdrawal

When declining mood begins to affects your sense of self-worth, your ability to deal with a situation, or you just don't want to deal with others offering to help – pulling away from people and causing self-imposed isolation, are signs of emotional withdrawl. As you become isolated from others and feel more alone, the negative thoughts and feelings you are dealing with will only increase to become a continued cycle of despondency. Emotional withdrawal is a sign of depression, one that people don't always recognize initially, as they may just see people giving reasons they cannot socialize.

Withdrawing from a person or situation can occur due to stress, burnout, frustration, or anger from what occurred. While different, withdrawal from people or activities you would normally enjoy is likely a sign of depression. Some who initiate self-imposed isolation may see themselves as not worthy of having or enjoying the benefits of relationships with others.

> **MONOTONE** – *I'm fine; I don't mind being at home and... it's fine. No, it's okay; I don't need to go anywhere, and I can get my own food (not doing this, losing weight). I have a lot of pain, but there is nothing I can do about it; whatever... my family is too busy anyway. I'm fine, I don't want to go out.*
>
> *– Edna S.*

These relationships will suffer from the emotional distance created, or changes from your previous personality, and the effects on family and friends will be great. Others may not understand how you are feeling and take your withdrawal as rejection. It can also be hard for others to see someone go through this hardship. Not everyone can be that friend or family member that is able to continue to support and encourage someone who is going through tough times, mostly because they cannot understand or don't know how they could help.

Addictions

What makes addiction so frustrating for people to cope with and resolve is that it can either be the cause of poor mental health or lead to someone's mental health decline. Either way, addiction can negatively impact all areas of your life. Having an addiction to a substance like drugs or alcohol is generally accepted as a medical diagnosis. Having an addiction to other activities like excessive video gaming or shopping is now widely accepted as a type of addiction. Regardless of what someone is dealing with, addictions are created by a need for pleasure, to escape, or distract from certain feelings or aspects of life.

Alcohol and drug addiction often cause individuals to do things that violate their own values and principles, as well as damage relationships with others. This disease creates the need for a substance, both physically and psychologically, past reasonable thought or the rational ability to refuse or ignore. It is a craving that is caused by physical, psychological, and chemical needs.

> **CRAVING** – *Alcohol used to be a way for me to manage my anxiety, which I didn't realize was all tied in together. I would be stressed at work and start to drink. I did it behind my family's back, and kept lying about what I was doing. They would catch me, and I'd promise to change—I really meant it at the time, yet I kept finding myself pulled back to it within a few weeks.*
>
> *– Sonia F.*

Individuals may have initially chosen to start taking a substance or engaging in an activity that wasn't optimal for them, but their subsequent behavior may not be by choice after becoming addicted to the feeling it provides. If you ever feel that you are unable to stop an activity or substance by your own choice, and it's becoming detrimental to your health or general ability to function with needed activities, seek out help immediately.

Addictions, like many signs of possible declining mental health, are quite toxic to both your personal and professional relationships. By addressing early any concerns you have for your mental health, you may be able to prevent the loss of good relationships, and work together to help you through ongoing difficulties, making these relationships a true place of strength and purpose for you both.

How to Improve Your Mental Health

There are numerous signs of declining mental health, many more than what has been mentioned thus far. When we talk about decline, we are referring to a change from your *normal* personality, where you are no longer able to function effectively in the care of yourself or for others in your charge. Depending on what you are dealing with and how severe your symptoms, seeking medical intervention may be required.

However, if you have identified the early stages of mental health dysfunction within yourself, there are several steps you can take to help improve how you feel, before you need to deal with significant medical intervention.

1. Exercise – I know, everything always leads to this, but for good reasons! Exercise produces hormones called endorphins, which provide us with natural methods to lift our mood, decrease pain symptoms, and make us feel motivated. Endorphins reduce feelings of stress, increase our immune response, and improve our sex drive. Exercise promotes socialization and provides a level of distraction from continually overthinking things.

Toxic Relationship with Your Mental Health

2. Healthy food choices – When we eat, we feel pleasure from the entire aspect of eating— smelling, seeing, tasting, and feeling content when our stomach is full. We often retreat to comfort foods when we feel bad, but they don't often make us feel better after we've finished them. While occasionally reaching for fatty, salty, or sugar-laden food items may hit the spot, generally, these types of foods make us feel worse after ingestion.

   Eating a diet with healthier options like fruit, vegetables, omega-3 fats, and lean protein, provides our brain with vital nutrients for improved brain function and mood. Providing our brain with the essential vitamins that it needs in order to grow, also ensuring that the brain to body functioning is working optimally. Healthier food choices are beneficial for stomach bacteria, which is good for both body and brain functioning, including your immune system.

3. Talk to a friend or family member (one that can listen to how you are feeling in a non-judgmental manner). Often, people start to feel isolated and just need to express how they are feeling. At other times, dialogue may be back and forth, and the other person can provide a different perspective of options, even a shoulder to cry on.

4. Socialization – Feeling less alone and not hibernating in your home may be one of the best methods to prevent further feelings of depression or other conditions. Distracting yourself from over-thinking and obsessing over emotions and other thoughts that may be going through your mind, and reminding yourself that you are not alone and that there are other good things in life, helps you maintain balance with your feelings.

5. Sleep – Insomnia has long been linked with people who have various mental health issues, including anxiety, depression, and OCD. It makes sense really; all these illnesses have an

excessive worry aspect to them, which affects our ability to enter a night of deep sleep. Without the ability to sleep and repair both our bodies and minds at night, regulating stress hormones and giving us time to recharge, we leave ourselves susceptible to worsening feelings about ourselves and others.

6. Avoid certain people or circumstances that promote poor choices—Don't be around that person (or people) who is not a positive influence on your mental health. Others who influence or pressure you into bad habits, make you feel worse about yourself, or contribute to your feelings of poor self-worth, need to be removed or limited in your life—this may include family.

7. Set goals – Have a plan and create a destination. Make an agreement with yourself to achieve something positive, and work hard to keep it. A goal gives you clarity on what you want to attain for yourself. It helps you identify the issue and makes a clear path for *you*, towards *your* solution. These goals may be small ones at first, but doing so can give you a sense of accomplishment, one that makes it easier for you to start taking larger steps forward in your mental health journey.

8. Journal – Self-reflection is very helpful for many people, as it keeps you honest and accountable to how you are feeling and what you want to accomplish. It can relieve stress by organizing your thoughts and allowing you to review how you feel and what goals you have set for yourself. It can help unburden your thoughts, without having to share them with another person. It can also explore your emotional response on a deeper level, thus giving you greater insight into who you are and how you got where you are now.

9. Hobbies (ones that you enjoy, which distract from poor feelings about yourself or others) – These can provide you with feelings of self-worth and accomplishment, as well

as provide a means to decrease stress. There are many hobbies that can be done individually or with others, which can provide another reason for healthy socialization.

10. Professional intervention/medication – If the above suggestions are not working for you, or it becomes obvious that you need a higher level of support, it's time to seek out an assessment from your doctor. Having a thorough assessment, and explaining to a professional how you feel, is the first step. If it is determined that you have a mild mental illness, monitoring and medication management may be well-controlled by follow-up appointments with your family doctor alone. If, however, it is identified that you require more support, a team approach with a psychiatrist, psychologist, or social worker may also be required, with a closer evaluation of how the medication is working for you, and more frequent visits.

Throughout life, we all need emotional support to get through difficult times in our lives, but sometimes these needs are greater than others. By learning healthy strategies on how to help yourself, or knowing when to turn to others, you may be able to avoid mounting emotional distress. Declining mental health leads to worsening coping ability and the increased likelihood of choosing poor coping mechanisms—excessive drinking, eating poorly, declining relationships, and many other toxic behaviors.

Lean on family and true friends; learn when you need help and when it's time to talk. Self-reflect on how you're really feeling and how you want to change a bad situation. Have that supportive network of friends and family you can rely on. Seek out professional assistance when your own actions are not enough.

Now that we have talked about how we can experience toxic relationships within ourselves, let's turn to some of the physical elements, where you may be demonstrating toxic behaviors in how you care for yourself physically.

CHAPTER 6

Toxic Relationships with Your Body (Physical Health)

To achieve all your desired goals in life, there is a priority relationship you need to foster, and that is the attention and melding of both your mental and physical health. When one of these aspects is ignored or not given the care it requires, an imbalance in our health occurs, negatively impacting both short and long-term health. When your health is poor, there is no opportunity or motivation to achieve other goals you want for yourself.

Throughout this book, we have focused on toxic relationships and how you can manage them. However, the longest and most important relationship you have is the one you have with yourself, and how you treat and nurture your mind and body. Self-neglect, even without intent, is the worst toxic relationship you can create, with extremely negative consequences to living your best life.

In the previous chapter, I focused on how important it is to take care of our mental health, the importance of self-care, and being open to ask for help when needed. Additionally, we discussed actions on how to get the assistance you need, to see you through tougher times. Let's now focus on the physical aspects of self-care, and how you always need to keep your relationship with your physical health one of your top priorities to ensure a long, *quality* life.

The Benefits of Physical Self-Care

In order to illustrate the points that we are about to cover, let's consider how our cars work and how they require regular ongoing maintenance. Your automobile has a variety of components that need to be cared for in order to get the best use out of it. Ignore oil changes and, eventually, your car's motor will seize up, and you'll have to deal with the cost of a major repair. If you don't maintain the air in your tires, you will eventually have a flat tire, which will leave you stranded on the side of the road. Lack of maintenance on your car can cost you money and lead to a dangerous accident—it may also lead to having to buy a new car.

Our bodies work in similar ways, except we don't have the ability to get a new one if we cause it permanent damage. If we damage our knees with poor use or years of excessive weight gain, they won't ever be the same again—even with possible surgery. If you eat high cholesterol foods your entire life, medication won't eradicate clogged arteries and poor circulation to your legs. There are many good reasons why a healthy body improves our enjoyment and quality of life, but yes, it does take effort.

Feeling Happy

Studies continue to tie the health of our bodies to the health of our minds. Clearly, when you move your body, through strenuous activity or exercise, it creates a distraction, but it's more than that. Exercise itself is doing something inside your body to decrease emotional and mental stress, but how?

When you exercise, your body releases hormones that elevate your mood, one of which is called endorphins. When endorphins circulate throughout your body, you feel better; troubles in your life seem less significant, and your mind is allowed a release from stress. This feeling can be like a rush of happiness and peace, where things don't seem as bad, and solutions to problems become clearer. If you can condition your body into wanting this positive feeling regularly, instead of seeking out destructive choices for solace, you can create a great outlet for everyday stress in your life.

Improved Confidence

A healthy body, one you are happy with, will increase your confidence to tackle many other goals and challenges in your life. When you are able to work towards and attain goals you can control, namely the health and fitness of your own body, you can use this same motivation to positively impact other aspects of your life.

Mental resilience is often tied to the strength and confidence you feel physically. The more you accomplish with physical fitness and good health, feeling and looking healthy, the more confidence you can feel towards tackling other obstacles.

Confidence comes when you can successfully deal with challenges. In your mind and heart, you now know that if you are faced with a similar situation again, you can successfully handle it. That same confidence can help you to take on more (healthy) risks in life because you recognize you can achieve goals and be successful, even when you are dealing with new situations or challenges.

Do something that scares or pushes you; try something you normally would not do—regularly. I have always believed that to grow as a person, to become confident in who you are, you can't be caged into the routine or boring. *Don't let anything hold you back from who you are meant to be! You deserve more for yourself!* Don't allow mediocrity to become your new norm when you want more!

This connection with optimal physical health and better mental health is huge, and trickles down to all other aspects of your life.

Improved Relationships

This improved confidence, and feeling good about yourself physically, will likely translate into your desire for healthy relationships with others, both romantic and platonic. Higher self-esteem decreases your risks for anxiety and depression, two things that cause many to withdraw from social settings and pull away from other people.

Having strong friendships gives us the opportunity to share ideas, challenge (in a friendly manner) each other on concepts, plus stimulate our minds and memories with different theories and beliefs. It improves cognitive functioning and supports longer-term memories, all important when you are in social settings and want to truly enjoy each other's company.

In working with seniors, regular social connections are very important to delay normal age-related memory decline. Additionally, those who have unaddressed hearing issues tend to be embarrassed because they can't hear conversations; subsequently, they start to pull away from others, causing further memory decline and social isolation.

A healthy and physically active body helps blood flow throughout our body and brain, providing us with healthy nutrients and oxygen, which improves cognitive functioning and performance. Improved energy and focus, plus body strength, occurs, with each system interconnected and supporting each other. What starts off with wanting a healthy, fit, pain-free body, leads to so many other quality gains for ourselves, our relationships, and others in our lives.

People are naturally drawn to those that give off positive energy, which is often tied to the self-assured feelings you have towards your physical capabilities and how you can manage your health. We will all have moments of challenge or weakness, but having an underlying strong body, functioning as well as possible, will go a long way to ensure that you can work through future health struggles.

Aging will lead everyone to eventually need to work through health challenges and new diagnoses, no matter how well we've treated our bodies. Having a manageable chronic disease, including neurological or autoimmune diseases, requires confidence and support from others— both in understanding how to manage them and understanding that you are not the only one out there dealing with health challenges. This prevents the isolating thoughts of *"why me?"* and replaces it with *"why*

Toxic Relationships with Your Body (Physical Health)

anyone?" What can WE do to work through our various health issues together, mitigating feelings of depression, isolation, or despair?

Many couples strengthen their relationship by incorporating physical activity into their time together. It allows couples to share and communicate in a setting that is outside their traditional home and work worlds. It also reinforces similar beliefs of health and joint couple goals, providing motivation and a shared healthy commitment to each other.

Your ability to care for yourself physically means that you are also setting a great example for your children, who often model the behaviors they see from their parents. The same benefits we as adults experience—improved confidence, learning to have relationships, and being part of a community—our children will learn from us as well.

Weight Management

As we age, changes in our bodies can make it more complicated and challenging to maintain a healthy weight. When you make physical activity and eating well a daily priority, you give your body the ability to do what is necessary to keep yourself in shape. Being fit and exercising regularly, on some level, does not mean that our only option is going to the gym. Working in our yards, going for regular walks, or doing a variety of other activities that make us move our bodies and weight-bear to promote circulation and to strengthen our muscles and bones, are all good. It's all about helping your body maintain the healthiest you possible.

Eating healthy does not mean you now have to live on super restrictive diets. Instead, make it about good food choices, more wholesome and less processed, that feed and enrich your body. If you want your body to work for you, then it needs to be fed the right nutrients throughout the day. The medical professional in me could go through a long list of healthy eating habits, but there is not one thing that is always good for every single person.

This is where knowing your own body, what it is sensitive to, what makes it function optimally and feel strong, is very important. For example, telling most people to eat more fruit is usually valid advice, unless you are diabetic, or have allergies or digestive issues—because then you must be selective. Making the right food choices for *you* will positively affect your physical body. Making regular healthy choices day after day will have a positive impact on your livelihood and your quality of life long-term. Remember, we all want to live long lives, *but* we also want to live our lives without any preventable disease, free of pain, and without debility, enabling us to enjoy aging and still have fun.

If you do need to initially follow some type of diet with restrictions to reach your optimal weight, there are numerous diet options to consider. I have discussed diet and weight-loss strategies in more depth in my previous book, **You Deserve More: How to Reinvent Yourself at Any Age.** Being able to reach or come close to your ideal weight is great, but don't obsess about an actual number. Instead, be realistic with your goal—weight charts don't reflect the appropriate weight guideline for many people (in my opinion), so pick your own goals. More importantly, go by how your body feels: Is it strong? Are you active? Are you in pain? Do you have health issues that you can attribute to excessive weight or lack of movement? Can any health issues be decreased or eliminated with weight loss?

The scale is just one method of keeping you on track, but it doesn't show what's going on inside your body. Someone with a 'healthy' weight and body appearance might have many health issues that are genetic or created due to poor health choices, such as poor eating habits or lack of exercise, but it isn't obvious to other people on the outside. We tend to judge people who have obvious weight gain, but many overweight people can be much healthier overall than their thinner counterparts.

Energy and Memory Alertness

If you consider that your brain is another muscle in your body, you can imagine that any benefits your body receives from good physical health, also benefits your brain. When you move your body, your heart pumps blood and oxygen throughout your systems, including your brain. Increased circulation additionally moves hormones through your body that contribute to happiness, alertness, and decreased stress.

Increased focus and energy, better sleep patterns, and improved circulation can all be attributed to physical exercise (even 30 minutes a day) and a resulting improvement in the physical functioning of your body. Better sleep allows us to have deeper sleep patterns, so you feel more refreshed and alert throughout the day. When you feel well-rested and happy, you will feel energized to accomplish many of the goals you want for yourself, including continuing physical activity to support that feeling of well-being.

> **STAMINA** – *I now wake up much faster and don't need to snooze my alarm four times anymore. I think I just get better sleep. Exercise does seem to help, because my body feels tired at night and I don't wake up throughout the night anymore.*
>
> *– Jenny J.*

Immune Health and Acute or Chronic Illness

Your immune system and its functioning are interwoven with all other systems in your body. When one system falters, it affects other systems as well. Having a healthy and well-functioning physical body is thought to have a direct effect on our ability to fight off disease. The intricacies of how a healthy body with regular exercise directly affects our immune system continues to be studied, but it only makes sense that someone coping with disease may have trouble fighting off infections. After all, how many things can your body truly do, all at the same time?

> **RESISTANCE** – *I've noticed that my husband gets sick more often. He used to be the one who never got sick from our kids, never got colds or coughs. Now that he's gained some weight, is on medications for high blood pressure and cholesterol, he's almost always the first one that gets sick. I didn't realize how immune*

health and general health were so tied in together. I wish he would start exercising again.

– Anna T.

Regular exercise contributes to a healthier cardiovascular and circulatory system, decreasing your risk for heart attack, stroke, and circulation issues in your legs. It can result in the improved functioning of many organs in your body, to decrease the risks for diabetes, kidney disease plus improve skin appearance, the function of your gastrointestinal system, and so much more. All areas of your body will benefit from the good effects of regular exercise and a healthy functioning body.

Clearly, all these benefits are going to positively impact your mental health. As I mentioned in the last chapter, there are many actions and choices that you make throughout your life that can positively impact your mental and physical health. I want to be clear that there are going to be challenges that are outside your ability to manage on your own. Yet by opening yourself up to the help that is available, you can address these challenges successfully.

For good physical self-care, you might need to unlearn bad habits that were modeled for you when you were young. Looking for resources to help you in that shift is one of the ways that benefit you mentally, because you won't put yourself down for what you do not know.

Now that I have focused on the benefits of good physical care, let's talk about what happens when you choose to ignore the needs of your physical body, or simply choose to burn the candle at both ends without recharging your personal physical batteries.

Signs Your Physical Health is Declining

Depression – Remember, exercise generally makes you feel happy, due to hormones released with physical activity, which last well beyond the actual activity. When we don't experience regular physical activity, day

Toxic Relationships with Your Body (Physical Health)

to day stressors start to build up, since we don't have an outlet to get rid of these feelings. If we start to feel unhealthy or guilty, or experience weight gain or increased pain, any of these and more will decrease our mood and can lead to depressive feelings.

Increased aches and pains – Part of any lack of physical care is how your body's level of pain will increase. When your body doesn't get the right level of exercise, your body will start to hurt just doing normal daily activities. Eventually, it turns into a level of chronic pain that leaves you vulnerable to other issues, such as further decreased activity, a dependency on pain killers or other poor methods to manage your pain.

> **DISCOMFORT** – *My back pains have come back again, and I know it's because I rarely exercise anymore. I used to be in much better shape last year, but since my trainer moved away, I haven't done any exercise regularly lately. I know I need to do something again. I used to feel so much better, younger, and healthier. Now I feel my age.*
>
> *– Samantha A.*

Increased use of drugs and pharmaceuticals – This may be attributed to many factors—pain, depression, or disease progression—leading to increased use of prescription or over-the-counter medications, or an elevation in alcohol or drug use. People may see that they are now dependent on many medications in order to function optimally, or seek out unhealthy methods to manage pain, depression, or a poor coping ability. If you're a smoker, you may see your cigarette use increase as a form of distraction or due to your poor coping and stress. You may even start up smoking again if you had previously quit

Declined circulation – When we move, all parts of our body benefit from muscles contracting and blood flowing from lower extremities to the brain and back down again. When we don't move, however, blood tends to pool in our lower legs and feet, causing swelling, pain, and risks for skin breakdown and chronic illness.

Decreased sex drive – Exercise has proven to increase desire, pleasure, and performance in your sex life. Improved circulation and muscle strength increase endurance, stamina, and desire, so you have a desire for sex, plus have the ability to follow through.

> **DESIRE** – *Oh, we don't do that anymore (laughs). I mean, sometimes, sure, yes. But we are so tired at night. And even he's not in the mood anymore. It's not the same anymore as we've gotten older and don't have the stamina now. He gets tired so quickly and has a heart condition. No, we don't exercise anymore. I know we could take regular walks but haven't done that for a while.*
>
> *– Tina F.*

Poor hair, nail, and skin quality – Poor nutrition and lack of vitamins and nutrients can be associated with hair loss, brittle nails, and dry or even overly oily skin. High-stress levels, which could have an appropriate outlet through exercise, can also attribute to these issues. When so much of your body requires healthy nutrients to function, these three areas tend to receive the least of what's available.

> **MANE** – *I'm going bald; do you see this bald spot in the middle? I recently cut my hair, so its weight is less, and my hair is easier to style. Look here, it's almost my skull here. You should see how much hair falls out in the shower now, so I only wash my hair twice a week. I am starting to eat more fruit and less sugar; more water seems to be helping also.*
>
> *– Sharlene R.*

Digestion issues – Lack of movement or exercise, and poor eating habits, can attribute to many physiological changes to our bodies, including constipation, diarrhea, intestinal and stomach aches, ulcers, and heartburn. Excess food intake is also not tolerated well by our bodies, like excessive sugar or processed foods. This causes an inflammatory response in our gastrointestinal (GI) tract that may now be linked with

Toxic Relationships with Your Body (Physical Health)

chronic health issues and cancer. Our GI tract (gut) processes food so that we can absorb nutrients for our body to function. Without the right nutrition or the ability to move food through our gut, we risk significant declining physical health.

> **CONSTIPATED** – *I've always had issues with constipation and never liked the taste of water, but I started gaining weight and knew I needed to finally do something. So, I started drinking water with lemon, and cutting back on sugar and bread—not all of it, but I want to be healthier. Can you believe I already lost 4 pounds in the last week? I'm so much less bloated, and started having bowel movements without laxatives.*
>
> *– Jane F.*

Poor sleep quality – Eating foods that cause an inflammatory response in our GI tract, means that our GI system is unable to function properly to break down and secrete hormones that help us sleep. Our stomach is our body's primary producer of serotonin, which is the hormone responsible for good sleep and mood. Poor sleep leads to less energy, less motivation, and less socialization, all of which have been proven to be beneficial to both your physical and mental health.

Memory decline and disease process – This may be the first symptom that can be attributed to declining health status. Body imbalances that cause bladder or respiratory infections, sepsis, or general infection, can directly cause decreased memory and focus. New memory decline can be associated with any number of acute or chronic illnesses, including Alzheimer's, Parkinson's, various neurological diseases (e.g., Huntington's disease), or uncontrolled thyroid and diabetes, to name just a few. And as we previously discussed, when we exercise and have a healthy cardiovascular system, oxygen flows more efficiently to our brain, improving it's functioning. Overall, an unhealthy body leads to a higher risk of memory decline, some preventable disease and worsens chronic progressive diseases. and various diseases in general.

The next part of this chapter is about how you can create change and thus put yourself in a place where your physical relationship with your body is one of peace and self-care.

Creating Change to Remake Yourself, for Your Best Physical Self

1. *Be honest about how you feel.* What hurts, feels stiff, or holds you back physically from obtaining goals you would like to achieve? Are you overtired, overstressed, or feel ill? Do you ignore symptoms of poor health or discomfort, afraid to learn the truth or simply don't want to take the time to find out what's happening? You're not alone by far, but that doesn't mean it's okay. Be in tune with your body. Pay attention when something doesn't feel right, gives you indigestion or headaches, affects your gut, and prevents you from experiencing what you want in life. These are all symptoms of something adverse happening in your body. You want to know what is happening so that you can be the best *you* possible!

2. *Get a physical.* If you are not one to have regular check-ups with your doctor, then you are overdue. Part of this assessment will include a weight check, blood work, and further follow-up to discuss your results—essentially, establishing a baseline of how you are doing, so if things change in the future, you know how your body functioned previously. While I'm an advocate of getting regular physicals from your family doctor, that doesn't mean it has to be done each and every year if you are heathy.

   Being a nurse that frequently has chronic back and neck pain due to my many years working in this field, I personally have added regular massage, osteopath and chiropractor visits to my health routine—something I consider essential for my own quality of life. You should see your family doctor, specialist, or health team more regularly if:

Toxic Relationships with Your Body (Physical Health)

- You have any acute or chronic health conditions that need monitoring
- You are on prescription medication
- You feel ill, have new pain, or you know something is different with how your body is functioning (remember, you know your body better than anyone else)
- You need to talk about addiction or mental health issues
- You are due for a preventative health screening test due to your age or family health history
- You are due for immunizations or are traveling somewhere they are required

3. *Regular dental check-ups for maintaining your gums.* Depending on your insurance coverage, if any, I know many people will find this expensive. That being said, prevention again is key, so while a dental check-up and cleaning may cost you money out of pocket, ignoring painful teeth or gums will cost you much more in the end with the inevitable fix-ups needed. Healthy teeth and gums are vitally important— obviously, first, just because we all must eat.

   Second, pain to your mouth area is going to greatly affect how you feel, and will trickle down to every aspect of your life. Ignoring tooth decay, gingivitis (gum inflammation), or periodontitis (bone and fibers are affected), greatly increases your chances of having a stroke or heart attack, as bleeding gums provide an entryway into your body for bacteria. Endocarditis (where heart valves and tissue are damaged by germs) is a life-threatening disease that has also been linked with people who have poor mouth hygiene and health.

4. *Exercise – cardiovascular and strength training.* It *always* goes back to exercise, right? Well, for good reason, as we so

often hear *"use it or lose it,"* but it's so true! It's also true that both are needed. Cardiovascular exercises (e.g., walking, jogging, tennis, swimming), those activities that make us sweat or breathe heavier, burn the most calories and keep our heart and circulatory system moving blood most effectively throughout. Weight-bearing exercises, however, create strong muscles and bone, producing longer-term effects that support our metabolism even when we sleep, as muscles burn calories even at rest. It stands to reason then, the more muscle you have, the higher your metabolism. The combination of doing these activities, three to five days per week, for at least 20–30 minutes, will create a stronger body—one better able to fight disease and infection, giving you the best quality of life.

5. *Eat and drink healthier.* Our bodies require certain nutrients to maintain health and prevent disease, needing a balanced diet of protein, carbohydrates, omega-3 fats, vitamins, and minerals. What are you getting now, and what food or vitamins need to be incorporated into your diet going forward? We all have different body compositions, levels of activity, food likes/dislikes, health issues, and heredity predispositions.

   While I could literally fill a book talking about all the different diets I have tried, and what has worked/not worked for me as well, there are four suggestions I feel comfortable in advocating—especially if your intention is to lose some weight, and you don't have health issues requiring specific oral intake.

   - Eat/drink fewer overall calories per day. (It is more important than the type of diet you follow—low carb, high fat, moderate fat, and many other combinations).

   - Increase your water consumption to over 1L per day (unless your doctor has put you on a fluid restriction).

Toxic Relationships with Your Body (Physical Health)

- Ensure adequate fiber intake to support regular bowel movements (through fruits, vegetables, grains, legumes and/or supplements).

- Mix it up, and don't eat the same thing all the time, or you will become bored and give up—be open to try new foods, spices, and methods of cooking.

- Prepare your meals ahead of time, don't be hungry without a plan, or inevitably you will eat poorly. Have healthy snack options on hand.

These suggestions, combined with some form of regular exercise, have been my most effective recipe for a healthier me. Can it be for you as well?

6. *Reduce stress.* Having a normal amount of stress in life is expected; we may even function better as it motivates and challenges us. Continually functioning in a high state of stress is both physically and emotionally detrimental, and has been proven to contribute to chronic diseases. This affects both work and family relationships, and may lead to mental health issues like depression and anxiety.

    Instead, it is important to focus on other activities that remind you of the fun parts of life, knowing that some stress will always be there but should not consume all your thoughts. Get out more with friends and family, and enjoy activities that have you exposed to sunlight and allows you to take in natural vitamin D, which often boosts mood. Join activities you enjoy doing, or take the time to discover a hobby you might love. Better nutrition, sleep, and exercise will also help. Find the FUN in your life and what works for you!

7. *Improve relationships with your significant other.* I will be honest; I'm a romantic at heart, and it is a shame that I didn't marry someone that was equally the same way. That

being said, we work around this by giving to each other, at different times, what each other needs. Otherwise, we could not be together and overall quite happy after 27 years of marriage. No relationship is perfect, and no two people are supposed to be exactly alike. But if you're in a relationship that primarily you are *not* happy in, most of your life will be consumed by this. It will likely detract from your motivation and joy in being able to achieve other goals in your life as well. Consider what aspects of your relationship can be improved upon and get both of you onboard.

8. *Improve communication with your children.* Who doesn't want this, regardless if they are young, teenagers, or adults with their own families? Having a good relationship with your children removes major potential stress in your life, allowing you to truly appreciate each other and understand how each is evolving as they grow and become more independent. Being able to work towards a mutual mature relationship, no longer treating your adult child as a child, should be the future goal for everyone. So as different aspects and stages in life arise, you can both benefit from the ongoing respect, love, and support everyone requires.

9. *Keep those who support you close.* Keep in better contact with friends and extended family who are there for you and with whom you share mutual respect and trust. It takes effort on both your parts, but those that add value to your life are the people you want when you have times of worry or health decline, and they can motivate you to achieve more for yourself. Good friends can go a long way to prevent mood and health decline, as they provide an outlet for stress and a reminder of the joys in life.

10. *Set goals for yourself and commit to them.* Start by listing out all the goals that you physically want for yourself. Laying them out can help you visualize where you want to focus your efforts—and be specific. Then start picking one

Toxic Relationships with Your Body (Physical Health)

thing at a time, and commit to this practice before adding more things on to it. Is it taking the dog for a walk every day, bringing your lunch to work, or cutting back on specific sugary drinks or foods? Is it learning to cook healthier food while incorporating more fruit and vegetables into your diet? Once you make that part of your routine, start adding more goals important to you, things that are achievable and motivating to continue leading you to your next accomplishment.

Another aspect of setting any goals is defining what might be holding you back. There may be a variety of reasons you are not currently practicing good physical self-care. By defining those challenges, you can start to brainstorm potential solutions to deal with those challenges. As you continue to meet small goals, you will be motivated to keep going. Plus, the benefits are going to start showing up, and that is motivating as well. My previous book, **You Deserve More: How to Reinvent Yourself at Any Age**, helps guide you step by step to learn how to set and follow through on all desired personal goals, including health—how to identify them, find time for them, and prioritize their importance.

11. *Motivate someone you care about.* Being able to motivate someone else you love, to fulfill their own fitness goals, will prove to be very motivating to yourself as well. Whether it's your spouse, children, sibling, or a good friend, you will have the added benefit of feeling better about yourself as well. Not only are you helping someone you care about, but you will also be reinforcing why you should continue doing the same. Having a health or workout buddy, someone who you can regularly join or talk/text with to keep each other motivated, is great to keep you both on task.

There are a variety of goals that you can create for yourself or with someone else to mutually support and benefit each other. Being overwhelmed with all the things you *could* do, then procrastinating on what you know you *need* to do, is truly the most difficult part of this journey. It is important to identify appropriate goals for yourself and carve out the time you need to accomplish them. Continue to learn and explore what is important for your body and mind, to ensure that you, and others, get the most out of life. Ultimately, the results you can achieve will be ongoing, and the benefits of being in overall better physical health cannot be stressed enough!

Now let's talk about the next form of toxic relationships you may encounter—one you may not have considered—how social media can become a toxic element in our lives.

CHAPTER 7

Recognizing Toxic Social Media, and Limiting Their Influence

Social media is now ingrained as a normal part of our everyday life. We find it hard to remember life without it, and that's nearly impossible for the younger generation to imagine—yet it's only been around for the last 22 years, since the advent of Six Degrees in 1997[4]. In the mid-1990s, AOL (American Online) was taking off, Yahoo had begun to set up shop, Amazon started selling books, and every home now needed a computer. The days of visiting the local library to research papers and homework, as it was done in the late 1980s, had begun to decline. More sites started to pop up, created to connect other people with similar and shared interests.

The social media space took the biggest step to becoming what we now know today. The launch of Friendster, in 2002, promoted the idea of a rich online community that exists with those who have common bonds[5]. From there, competition formed with new social media sites,

---

4   Hendricks, D. (2013, 5 8). *Complete History of Social Media: Then And Now*. Retrieved from Small Business Trends: https://smallbiztrends.com/2013/05/the-complete-history-of-social-media-infographic.html

5   *Friendster*. (n.d.). Retrieved from Wikipedia: https://en.wikipedia.org/wiki/Friendster

including Myspace, Facebook, LinkedIn, and more. As various social media platforms began to merge, their desirability and audience continued to grow. Today, instead of picking up a phone book, we connect with others via various social media platforms and email—and our smartphones are never far out of reach, keeping us constantly connected.

What a difference the last two decades has seen in the world of social media, and to the internet itself. Today, kids are known for their attachment to texting, and those born in the 2000s are the first generation to be raised with social media from the start. There are social media platforms to now address every type of interest, from connecting with family, to reaching out for business, through video game mediums—and don't forget dating sites. There are platforms that allow you to play games, promote businesses, create various social groups, and share your thoughts, with little effort and via many devices.

This ability to express every idea and give or gain information instantly has created its own challenges. With the ability to adopt an online persona, previous traditional filters have disappeared, and a layer of perceived anonymity has encouraged us to express our opinions in ways that would be unacceptable face-to-face. With this freedom, however, comes the risk and development of the current climate of online bullying, illegal activity, and the spread of lies and inaccurate information.

Another aspect of social media is how it has played into the world of capitalism. Using various types of behavior tracking mechanisms, companies can now target their products more effectively than with paper flyers. Marketing companies have been created to produce content meant to grab your interest and direct you to advertisers that provide the products and services you're more likely to be interested in. Excessive hype, ease of access, and focused attention are reshaping how we shop and spend. Online advertising is not your typical television commercial, newspaper ad, or billboard.

Recognizing Toxic Social Media, and Limiting Their Influence

With increasing technology and social media opportunities, both for personal and professional gain, there are many discussions on how this is affecting our relationships with others. Too many of us are guilty of going to dinner and spending more time on our phones than in conversation with anyone at the table. Studies are also in progress that look at the developmental impact of our growing ties and dependence on technology.

Clearly, there are many benefits and concerns associated with our use of social media. Let's first explore some of the benefits and how it is being used in a positive way to create social change.

The Benefits of Social Media

The beauty of social media, at its core, is the ability to help individuals connect with other people, whether they be old friends or new. Think about how many members of your family you currently keep up with through social media platforms. You share photos, send updates on big events, and in some cases, share struggles and sad events with people you know. Birth announcements, deaths, accomplishments, and funny or sad news save hours of phone calls, with potentially hundreds of friends and family members.

There are many other benefits to social media. When we are looking for recommendations for a product or service, we can get nearly instantaneous feedback from family and friends, just by asking others through these platforms. The other point of connection is the ability to rally people to a cause or issue, simply by spreading the word through a simple post. The share button is key to connection and growth.

As things continue to go viral, some have built thriving careers around their ability to create subject matter that others enjoy. Merchants also recognize the value of creating content that connects with their target audience. In fact, they pay a small fortune for the privilege of having influencers review their products and services. For many of us, finding out about these products and services starts with content that allows us to click on a website where we can place an order. All of that can happen from our phone or computer, with only a few simple clicks. Social media platforms have become an all-encompassing way to build relationships, market goods, and create momentum for a variety of causes.

Then there are social media applications offering opportunities to meet new people with similar interests, goals, and dreams—think of all the social groups that have evolved. As people with similar interests continue to connect around the world, new cultural connections have also occurred. People are learning more about others all the time, particularly those that might live thousands of miles away.

These new relationships have made the world smaller in some ways, yet larger in others. Social media has allowed everyone to travel the world, see new sights, and explore their interests. Love connections have been made between people who may have never met if not for the internet and social media's wide range. People are building lives and families across geography and culture. This is an amazing part of the world of social media.

Even when you are primarily connecting with people who live and work in your area, social media has become a news source and informational hub to spread critical information about a variety of things—school and local events, advertisements for business, and the ability to build awareness of community issues. Think of how parents, teachers, and sports groups have created private social media groups, sharing pictures from classrooms and sports events, specifically targeted to a closed group. Many parents find this appealing because it's confidential, keeps them up to date, and prevents the need to track or find any paperwork.

The government has also taken to social media, using it to share information regarding deadlines for taxes, voting information, road closures, and important information its citizens need to know. The fast communication speed means information can be spread quickly, without needing to wait for the local news cycle to occur.

Recognizing Toxic Social Media, and Limiting Their Influence

All this information, relationship connections, and fun exploration on social media, means that we can spend hours taking advantage of all the various options available. It can be so easy to use your phone at any time of the day, whether you're relaxing or engaged in a less appealing activity.

Let's discuss the other side, the side that includes the many challenges and potential problems or dangers that social media can create.

The Potential Toxic Aspects of Social Media

The issue that many of us have come to recognize is the ease with which social media can quickly consume much of our time and energy. You can easily become emotionally drained as you flip through the various pictures and stories of other individuals. While many of us recognize that our own lives are far from perfect, we can be quick to believe that the carefully curated photos, stories, and videos that other individuals post are true about their own lives.

As you compare your own imagined flaws and shortcomings against those 'perfect' images, it can lead to negative feelings. Any constant flow of adverse thoughts can leave you feeling sad or questioning your own self-worth, leading you to constantly compare yourself with others. Many people get sucked into others' false worlds, thinking they cannot measure up to what others have or are experiencing. This can lead them further towards feelings of depression and anxiety due to the influx of information from this constantly inflated world.

> **FALSE WORLDS** – *It must be nice for them to get away and go on a trip. All I've seen is her pictures of exotic places, and it must have cost a fortune. I'll never have enough money to go to places like that. I work two jobs, and it will never be enough.*
>
> *– Sarah T.*

While individuals may at times share negative comments or experiences, it is more common for most of us to share only happy events. Keep in mind, depending on how far-reaching your social media contacts are, there are people who will only share untruths and exaggerations, people who are even paid to do so! False or inaccurate information tends to spread quickly through social media. People often become overly invested in arguing over information or stories posted, only to find out later that it wasn't even accurate. Do your due diligence, and don't blindly believe everything that is posted.

> **MISLEAD** – *I thought that actor was dead! The story said he died in his sleep a few weeks ago—drugs I think. How horrible for someone to create a story like that and advertise it. Isn't there some regulation against fake stories?*
>
> *– Sharon D.*

There is also a changing manner of how people communicate when using social media. As was briefly mentioned, the natural filters that most of us have when dealing with individuals in person may disappear as soon as we sit behind a keyboard. The old saying that "words cannot hurt you," is no longer true. In fact, not only do words hurt, but they linger and are far-reaching, having possible extreme social, professional, and legal ramifications. How many public figures today regret what they did, many years later, after pictures surfaced on social media? What might you regret if there was a picture of you to surface in the future?

Bullying through social media, especially that which affects teenagers, has become rampant and far more difficult to deal with than the physical altercations of the past. The ability to avoid people who would yell or physically harm you is still there, but the attacks can easily continue online. In the past, you could physically avoid the bully or retreat to the safety of your home, but that is no longer the case. Online harassment can be observed by a very large audience, and many will not feel any respite from their persecution.

> **TORMENT** – *We were just joking around; he posted a good picture of himself, but he's trying to show off his abs, so of course*

Recognizing Toxic Social Media, and Limiting Their Influence

we're going to make fun of him! It was hilarious, and we could not help ourselves. We kept commenting on his appearance and comparing him to 'dad body' celebrities as a joke. He was a bit offended, and the comments continued even when he tried to delete the post.

– Samuel M.

Don't think that online bullying only affects children; many adults, and specifically media personalities, are targeted by others through many forms of social media. Trolls, or those who target and try to upset others on social media, are rampant on the internet, and hide behind their anonymity. Strong opinions, falsehoods, threats, and fake photos or videos may be used by others to harass and bully other adults online.

How can all this impact your health? Clearly, it can end up leading to profound anxiety and depression in some people. Additionally, if you are spending a significant amount of time online and using social media platforms, then you are not necessarily making those personal, face-to-face connections with other individuals. Think about how enjoyable it is to sit down with your friends and loved ones and have a great conversation. This emotional and physical connection to actual people is very important for brain stimulation and long-term memory.

Social media, while it can provide connections, can also promote loneliness. If you are alone in your home, rarely socializing with others in person, you can start to lose traditional face-to-face communication skills. Some would argue that this has become apparent with people who play video games excessively in their homes, as they have lost social skills and the ability to take part in normal day-to-day activities. Continually turning to social media can easily turn into one of your hobbies, instead of being the conduit to that hobby or to other people who share similar interests—causing more isolation and loneliness.

ALONE – *I like to read the articles on the stars, and see what they are doing. I like seeing their outfits and where they are going. It's a perfect life I think, getting to dress up and go on yachts and* *parties. It's not like I could ever do something like that, have a life like that. I'm fine with being at home. I don't mind it; I'm not really a social person anyway. I'm fine with my TV and computer.*

— Trish T.

Although some do not appear to mind being alone, others will find physical isolation very lonely, which contributes to anxiety and depression risks. Watching other's lives through the screen of a computer can make you feel as though your life isn't good enough, causing jealousy and despair. Limiting social media is important in preventing overload, especially in people with lower self-confidence who question their accomplishments.

Experts continue to point to the decline in basic communication skills, which is occurring simply because we constantly use short cuts when interacting via social media or text messages. The result is a decline in how we verbally interact. When not behind a phone or keyboard, they're finding it more challenging to say what they think face-to-face.

The impact of your communication skills directly impacts how others perceive and form any opinions of you. People who seem quite articulate when they talk may have very poor written skills. Social media is felt by many to be eroding our ability to spell, and use appropriate punctuation and proper grammar[6]. That communication has now evolved into many different formats, including texting, which tends to shorten words with the addition of emoji's and acronyms—something the younger generation has been born into. School assignments and professionals don't generally appreciate the overall change in writing and spelling ability for written documentation.

CORRODE – *Just look at your kids; through texting, we can't understand what they're saying. Even with my wife, I hardly know*

---

[6] Cowens, S. (2017, 4 28). *Spelling and Grammar in the Age of Social Media.* Retrieved from Math Genie: https://www.mathgenie.com/blog/spelling-grammar-social-media

what she's telling me. They swap out words with acronyms and expect me to know what they are typing. It's frustrating and takes too much effort to figure out what they are trying to say to me.

– Danny C.

And finally, relationships with family and friends will also be negatively impacted if someone is unable to put down the phone and disconnect from the constant pull of social media. This leaves them unable to focus on the person they are physically spending time with, and the result is that those friends and family members feel neglected and ignored, or just see them as rude.

There are a variety of areas where social media can become quite toxic, especially if left unchecked; therefore, it is important to look at your social media habits. Next, let's find ways to positively address any poor habits you've developed.

Finding Healthy Ways to Limit Social Media

We've acknowledged that social media has its many benefits, but if it becomes the primary focus of your life, negative effects can also show. If you are concerned that you are too wrapped up in what others post, or find yourself posting excessively, there are a few steps you can do to help be aware and decrease your usage.

1. Take advantage of the tools available on your phone or computer to track and restrict your usage. Understanding when and how much time you spend on social media platforms is important to help you address your habit.

2. Once you understand that, you can then start being intentional in deciding when you will spend time on social media. Schedule times in the day when you will look at or post content, chat with people, and comment on posts— but stick to a schedule so that other tasks can also get done.

3. If you are finding it difficult to stop turning to social media, identify what is happening in your day when you go to your device. Look for insight into how you are feeling and why you are doing this. For instance, are you feeling lonely, and do you look online to feel connected? Are you neglecting other aspects of your life, instead preferring to keep up with what others are posting?

4. Start scheduling more time with friends and family in person. Think of family dinners or lunch with friends as a sacred period where phones are off-limits. Find ways to connect with people outside social media portals, and allow yourself to address any possible feelings of loneliness and depression.

5. Plan family activities on weekends, where all technology is turned off and you simply enjoy activities together and each other's company. Times like these can create amazing memories while fostering social skills and strengthening relationship bonds.

Clearly, there are a variety of ways to lessen the negative impact of social media while continuing to allow yourself to enjoy the positive aspects of it. If you feel that you are excessively using social media, take the time to look for ways to shift yourself away from your online life, towards what you love to do, and those that you love to spend time with.

CHAPTER 8
Toxic Strangers

Our world today is full of thousands of interactions with strangers, both in person and through social media. Think of all the people you come into contact within the course of just one day. You could start your day with a few comments on a general social media post or blog, where you also read the comments of others. Then you head out the door, where you move past many different individuals as you travel to work, school and other places. Most of these people you barely notice, whether by car, walking, or public transportation. Some encounters can lead to a pleasant interaction, such as a smile or a thank you for a coffee, but others might leave you with a sour taste in your mouth. Your whole attitude for the day can be adversely impacted when you have unpleasant interactions, leaving you feeling angry, frustrated, or sad, even though you began in a pleasant mood.

Depending on your job or general routine, your day may include countless interactions with any number of relative or actual strangers— co-workers, clients, people from your child's school, random individuals on the street, in a store—anyone really. These interactions can include personal or work email exchanges, face-to-face meetings, and phone calls throughout the day. As you head into the evening, encounters may continue if you choose to go out to dinner with family or friends, have errands, or see people on your street as you enter your house.

As casual encounters occur with strangers and acquaintances throughout your day, each of these interactions has the potential to positively or negatively influence your mood. Perhaps you might have had a less than positive experience with an individual at the coffee shop or from another driver. Now you are in a bad mood that continues to negatively impact your interactions with others throughout the rest of your day.

Having positive energy and influence in our lives can help us protect ourselves from any negative interactions and their impact. When you are not focused on the positive, a brief negative contact can continue to bother you for hours, days, or many weeks afterward. Part of what is critical for us to consider is how to say no to those toxic interactions, and allow ourselves to be confident in dealing with various difficult exchanges. Knowing when to say no, when to go after what we want or need, and when to walk away from a toxic situation, is very important, especially when encountering unexpected situations with strangers.

> **HOSTILE** – *When I go out to a bar with my friends, I like to dance and have a good time. Once when I was drunk, I bumped into a guy on the dance floor. I'm a big, fun guy, but the other guy didn't accept my apology and started swearing and threatening me and my friends on the dance floor. After this guy started pushing my friend around, I reached for a beer and threw it in his face. While not the best move, it did shock him enough for a moment, and the bouncers moved in and decided to throw us all out. It thankfully prevented the potential for increased violence, and we continued our night somewhere else.*
>
> *– Aaron J.*

Part of your journey is determining for yourself whether an interaction is toxic. Can you determine this in a few moments? Depending on what it is and who, or what is occurring, you often have split seconds to decide. When is it worth pushing back, or just ignoring the situation so that it doesn't escalate or ruin your day? You don't want to be a victim, so you need to make quick judgments. Are there then moments when you should give someone another chance, allowing you to put a toxic moment in the past? What are some of the ways that you can be a source of positivity for others who may be in a toxic space or just looking to start a dispute?

Identifying Potentially Toxic Behaviors

Let's be clear; some people can be rude, no matter what you do or don't do to them—but even the most mild-mannered individuals can have moments when they are impolite or not at their best. Think of all the small ways people can be impolite without even thinking about it: not holding the door open when your arms are full of packages, or letting an elevator door close in your face. You might be driving down the road and be cut off by another car, or walking down the street and have rude comments shouted at you, or people ahead of you in line let others butt in line ahead of you.

Notice that each of these incidents can have the ability to wreck your mood, and in some cases, ruin your day. A shot of negativity can get us so focused on how we were wronged that we can't focus on anything else, causing great stress and turmoil within us. Tunnel vision sets in, which can impact your ability to focus on other tasks you need to accomplish. To keep these incidents from overtaking your day, it helps to be proactive.

When one of these incidents occurs, it is important to stop and take a deep breath. Recognize that these events likely have nothing to do with you personally. The individual might be having a bad day, be oblivious of their actions, or simply be an overall rude person. Pausing and taking deep breaths gives you a moment to clear your head. Explore your emotions for a moment, then make the conscious decision to let the incident go and not excessively rehash it in your mind. This gives you back the control over your day, and moves the incident to your rearview mirror.

There are a variety of toxic behaviors that can be found in daily interactions with strangers, where people are not falling in line with what is felt to be societal norms. Regardless of when they occur or who is involved, they can negatively influence you to the point that it clouds your entire day, week, or even impacts you for years to come. How many of us can remember an uncomfortable situation we encountered or observed, that even now we recall? I bet many of you have come across some of the examples below.

Road Rage

Road rage is one of the most common toxic stranger encounters we have to deal with at some point. These are situations that we've encountered or have seen between others, ranging from milder honking and hand gestures to car accidents or people getting out of their cars to fight. I wager that every one of you has at some point experienced or witnessed a situation that has upset you when driving on the road—whether you were annoyed, shocked, mad, yelled out your window, gave or received a rude gesture—but hopefully not a physical encounter. We likely have all had the potential to come across any number of road frustrations.

Road rage is a negative encounter that can quickly escalate. You may get cut off or do something in error yourself, but regardless of what starts the incident, it can escalate quickly if those involved do not exert some control over their emotions. While there are cases where one individual might turn around and act violently with little provocation, the truth is that most aggressive incidents require two people to escalate.

> **INDIGNANT** – *I still remember this driver, even five years later. She was driving so slow on the highway, way under the speed limit, and I had just gotten on the highway. I passed around her and went back into the right lane. I knew my turnoff was not far ahead. I did not cut her off and was well ahead, so there should have been no issues. A few minutes later, I see this car speed past*

me and narrowly cut me off, immediately veering to the off-ramp. It was so unexpected and it startled me. I looked towards the driver. The same slow driving lady was there, looking me right in the eye, giving me double fingers. I honked back but literally was so astounded I barely reacted. I could not believe she was pissed off at me! To this day, I still remember that and how much it bothered me.

– Hannah G.

Prevention of Escalation

How can you stop or diffuse a road rage incident? First, pause before speaking or reacting. Even if the other individual has done something wrong, deliberately or by accident, you still need to be in control of your own actions. By controlling your response, you are likely going to help de-escalate the situation. Take a breath and drive away if appropriate and there are no damages or injuries to report. Do not engage, even if insults are thrown at you. It is important to remember that this is likely a very small aspect of your day. Is being angry about the mistakes made on the road going to fix anything? Is it going to change what occurred? Prevent physical risks of harm, and swallow your pride, at least at that moment—it's not worth the consequences.

The truth is that getting angry and holding onto it just makes you feel awful. Be open to letting go of these feelings by acknowledging them and working through what happened. Could you have done anything yourself to have prevented this interaction? If your incident involves a car collision, then remain calm and do what needs to be done, involving your insurance companies and the police. You can never control how other people interact, but you can help de-escalate a potentially volatile situation and prevent a minor road rage incident or accidental collision from escalating into physical violence.

Verbal and Physical Aggression

Aggression occurs when it's directed at another person, where there is an intent to harm someone or something else that is sentimental to them. If you break an object that has no meaning, you are not articulating your emotions appropriately, but it would not be considered aggressive. If you break an object, knowing that it had deep meaning to another person, and to cause some type of emotional harm, this would be considered aggressive.

This type of behavior can be exhibited by another person exhibiting rudeness, intimidation, belittling, being disrespectful, or raising their voice. It can escalate into bullying behavior and physical violence in some situations, but day-to-day aggression is seen or felt all the time. It can include everything from someone slamming a door in your face, being yelled at, or being shoved out of the way on a busy street.

> **ENCOUNTER** – *A group of us went to the movies several years ago. Soon after we sat down, a group of teenagers came to sit right behind us and were loud and rowdy from the start. It took about ten minutes of my chair being kicked before the racket in my ears drove me crazy. Eventually I stood up, turned around to face them, and yelled for them to shut the hell up. The theatre heard and clapped at my action. I'm a big guy, so when I look upset, it usually makes people pause. Thankfully, this scared them enough that they didn't speak for the rest of the movie.*
>
> *– Wayne R.*

There are countless more incidents that can and do occur between people, most of which do not rise into increased verbal and physical aggression—but how do we know which situation will intensify and which will end with apologies? What can we do to prevent escalation?

Prevention of Escalation

You can't always foresee stranger encounters and the flare-up of tempers with people you don't know. It's not the same as talking to your colleague at work or your brother, where you know what to avoid saying or doing. The average person does not go out of their way to start an aggressive encounter, yet it happens. In fact, one person may do very little of anything, but the other person has churning emotions they are holding onto, just waiting for an easy outlet on the first available victim.

Not unlike what we've talked about with road rage, the number one thing you need to do is remain calm. If someone is being verbally aggressive toward you but does not present an immediate risk for violence, there are several things you should consider in these circumstances:

1. Remain calm.
2. Don't be within any range of being physically touched and harmed.
3. Evaluate your physical surroundings, in case you need to leave immediately.
4. If you did something in error, apologize to the other person.
5. Try to de-escalate the situation and talk about what occurred.
6. Add humor or change the subject as appropriate.
7. Report the incident if related to poor customer service.
8. Leave if there is a risk for escalating physical violence (no pride is worth any injury).

Online Dating

Of course, you want to make a positive first impression; we all do! And hopefully, your date does also. A first date is the first opportunity to really see if someone can be a good match. While it is easy for any of us to fantasize about what could be or how you want something to be, remember what is most important. It is not just about how you look or dress; you and they should be evaluating personality, emotional stability, and looking for general "creep" factors. Remember, you are meeting a relative stranger for the first time, face to face, so your job is to also evaluate your date for potential risks to yourself or warning signs of a toxic personality.

> **PREDATOR** – *I knew before I even met him that I would never meet him in person. I picked someone on a social media dating site that was not my normal type—he was more nerdy, dorky, and not initially attractive to me, but I decided to chat with him anyway. He was fun to text with and seemed really nice, sounding quite normal until we decided to get together for coffee. The night before we arranged to meet up, he started asking me questions like what positions I liked, escalating to asking me for a safe word because he's into fake rape and choking. No surprise, I never met or texted him again!*
>
> *– Brianna F.*

Online and first dates come with their own challenges. Online dating has become a very popular way to meet new people, for both long and short-term relationships. It has an ease of convenience that is hard to beat, and allows you to communicate with people you never would have met otherwise. There are also many negatives for these same reasons. You can often make quick judgments on people face to face, which is impossible through an online dating site.

It is easy to create a misleading profile and present an entirely different you, one that is nothing like the truth. The reasons for this are many, and not always for the worst reasons—lack of confidence and feelings of desperation are not uncommon, but there are also many liars, scammers, and predators with their own agendas. Don't share too much about yourself before you really get to know someone. For this reason, it is also important to always keep a few things in mind when meeting with someone for the first time.

Toxic Strangers

1. A little informal investigation on your part never hurts. With the abundance of information on the internet and through social media sites, you may easily come across something your potential date has done that would nullify them as being someone you would want to meet in person.

2. Let someone else know where you are going, who you will be with, and for how long. Arrange a call at the end of the evening to let a friend or family member know you are home.

3. Provide your own means of transportation to and from the date; don't be reliant on your date to get you home. This added benefit prevents a bad date, a person you don't want to see again, from knowing where you live.

4. Is it possible to arrange a double date with your friend? If not, always meet in a public place and do not allow yourself to be isolated; ensure that there are other people nearby in case you meet up with an undesirable person.

5. Know yourself, and don't try to make something happen just because you feel alone, isolated, or needy. You can't make something happen that isn't there. Additionally, if you feel that something is wrong, or this person exhibits traits not for you, heed your instincts and, without being rude, hasten the end of your date.

CREEPY – *I went on a first date with this guy, and from the beginning, I knew something was wrong. He was super late to start, then all he did was talk about his body and how much money he made. Soon into the date, he then started talking about how he'd buy us a house together—we had just met in person! He also had expectations: dinner ready when he got home, he'd put a few babies in me, and I needed to keep my looks up for work events. Before the end of the night, I called a friend to pick me up but got stuck sitting on a park bench, waiting for my ride. He* *kept inching closer to me till I was almost crying and falling off the bench. I could not wait to end that night!*

– Clementine R.

Evaluation of a first date means looking for signs of questionable behavior. Throughout this book, I have included different forms of toxic or negative behavior that should raise red flags. On first dates, do they want to talk over you or tend to push for their own wants or desires? Do they exhibit signs that your personal preferences are not as important as their own? How do they treat the wait staff or others that you encounter on your date? The point is to build an understanding of how they may treat you in the future, by studying how they treat those around you.

Recognize that you might not weed out every negative or toxic person on the first date, but you can start to recognize signs that may help you decide against a second date. Do not be too quick to judge someone, but instead assume that everyone is nervous and can say the wrong thing once, maybe twice—but multiple examples of these behaviors are red flags that should cause you to question pursuing this relationship.

At any time in life, you may run into strangers that give you uncomfortable feelings, so go with your gut instincts. At times, you might find yourself trying to ignore those instincts to avoid being rude; however, the most important thing is your own safety. Always be aware of your surroundings, avoid being cornered, never walk with your head down, and be aware of what individuals are around you. If someone starts to invade your space, be willing to walk away. Self-defense classes can also assist in keeping you safe regardless of the situation. Always do your best to maintain your safety by first preventing a bad situation.

Regardless of what you encounter, the most important thing to remember is that you want to avoid the type of negative self-talk that leaves doubts in your head. You want to feel good about how you handled the situation, regardless of how they reacted. Ultimately, you want to feel good about how you handle any meeting or encounter. After all, you can only control yourself, not those around you.

To be clear, you should never apologize if you did nothing wrong, but be willing to accept responsibility if you are at fault. Often, just acknowledging your role in the situation can help to defuse it. Feel confident in standing up for yourself if necessary, but recognize that even if you are correct, that doesn't mean the other person will acknowledge that you are right.

In fact, some people will want to argue and aggravate the situation, being unwilling to let go of their position. Sometimes choosing to let it go can be the best move and allow you to have peace. By acknowledging your part in creating the encounter, you are demonstrating that you can take responsibility for your actions. You have the power to control your thoughts and actions, so taking steps to do so can often help to defuse many of these negative situations.

No matter what happens, don't let these toxic situations ruin your day or dominate your thoughts for weeks or years to come.

CHAPTER 9
Always Forward, Never Back

My goal in sharing this information is to help you understand the different types of toxicity that can be found in various relationships within your life. It's critical to have the knowledge and tools to recognize those toxic elements, as well as the ability to act in a way that protects you. Part of this protection is about making conscious choices regarding boundaries, plus recognizing the toxic elements that may exist in a relationship before they become too damaging to either party.

If you're concerned that you, or someone you care about, is struggling with a toxic relationship, consider how you can focus on implementing what you have learned from our discussions. You should want more for yourself, or them, and explore what is causing the relationship to be destructive. Are there manageable and safe ways to improve on it, or is it time to remove yourself from the situation? Take charge of your life, and allow yourself to find joy instead of living in constant stress, anxiety, or fear from toxicity.

While considering if you are in a toxic relationship, ensure that you also don't create hostility towards others that might contribute to their poor health. Be a mirror of the personality you seek from others. Bring the enthusiasm, optimism, and encouragement that you want in your life to others.

The truth is, at some point in our lives, we have all likely contributed to demeaning someone else, and have *been* the toxic element to another person by creating emotional turmoil. While it may not have been a deliberate action with the intent to cause harm, it had the same effect, nonetheless. Using what we have discussed, you have the tools to now identify if you are the source of toxic elements in any of your current relationships. If you have identified some traits or tendencies in yourself, or if you find that a few people in your life are often subject to your sarcasm, mockery, or disrespect, then you are now in a position to find ways to correct those traits within yourself.

> **SCAPEGOAT** – *I'm not sure why he brings this out in me. I mean, he's a nice guy and sort of my friend, but he's also irritating. He's the one that our friend group makes fun of the most. It's a joke, of course, all in good fun. Yes, anyone can be made fun of, but it's usually him... No, I don't think he likes it anymore; maybe he never did. He gets upset sometimes, but it's hard to stop. He's such an easy target!*
>
> *– Sam H.*

It may not be easy to stop bad habits, but you must consider the ramifications of your own behavior on someone else's emotional health and self-confidence. This behavior may affect their future decisions and views on life in a profoundly long-term way. No one appreciates always being the butt of a joke, particularly by their closest friends or family members. Being aware and conscious of this is the first step toward helping you address and change those behaviors and attitudes in yourself. Greater awareness gives you the ability to create significant change. Moving forward, how can you ensure that you're not the toxic element in any of your current relationships?

Part of the journey for those wishing to improve their behavior towards others is self-reflection and the *want or will* to analyze what they are doing to themselves or others; for them not to hold themselves above self-scrutiny, and accept criticism, to want to learn from their mistakes and move past them—otherwise, there is no ability for self-growth and change.

What toxic behaviors are within those who are either the creator or the victim in a toxic relationship? With understanding and insight, anyone holding either role can make changes to their behavior for better health, both for themselves and others. While we know that the victim can be affected profoundly, we may not think about the instigator and what inner demons they are likely battling.

Do not think that a constantly negative, stressed, or angry person doesn't have the weight of their own mental health issues, which are destroying aspects of their own physical health as well. It may not be what we consider initially, since we want to help the victim—but if the toxic person is a family member or friend, why would you not want to free them from their demons as well? What's behind the curtain? Look beyond their actions, and seek an understanding of why they do what they do, in order to help them as well.

> **JADED** – *He's never happy anymore; he's always complaining about how people treat him and waiting for the next shoe to drop. I know he was babied by our parents growing up. He never had to work hard at anything as a kid, so when the reality of life hit him, it seemed like he couldn't cope! When my parents died ten years ago, he just seemed lost, angry, and bitter. How does he have money now, without their income? I think he steals and hangs with a lot of people I know have gone to jail. He still bullies my sister, the neighbors hate him, and his landlord wants him out... You'd never believe he used to be happy and social, always going out and had a lot of friends. I don't know if I care to try and help him anymore.*
>
> – *Mark C.*

You will often see similar personalities attracted to each other. Have you ever wondered why people who are the victim often have multiple relationships with people who take advantage of them? That a toxic or dominant personality, in turn, finds someone they can boss around? Some learn from a one-time bad relationship, while others continue to find the next similar toxic situation. Want more for yourself and others in your life; learn how you can prevent or remove yourself from relationships that allow you to be a toxic person, or allow others to be toxic to you.

Takeaways

Let's consider some takeaways and key thoughts on life, as we consider our current relationships and mindset.

1. Don't take things that happen in your life so personally. While it may feel like the world is against you some days, not everything in life happens as a direct assault on you. You are not the center of everything or everyone that touches your life. What people say and do often reflects on their own inner thoughts and turmoil, but rarely has anything to do with you. It is far more productive and healthier for you to just let go of others' opinions and be confident about who you are and what you can offer them. Operate from a place where your heart, wisdom, and intuition serve as a guide for your choices in life.

2. Be aware of the significant impact that negative thoughts can have on you, and how it can alter your personality and others in your circle. When you surround yourself with individuals who cannot or will not let go of negativity, you are only reinforcing your own negative thoughts. Do not become an individual who refuses to see the positive opportunities in life. Negativity leads to expecting and accepting the worst in people, almost ensuring that you don't believe you are worthy of more. It also leads you to believe that you should not reciprocate back to others, that it's not appreciated or wanted. When you then feel that you are unworthy of respect, love, compassion, and an equal

relationship with others, you are also unable to walk away from those who are toxic to you.

3. Recognize that constant complaining without action fuels a sense of victimhood. If you allow yourself to live in the world as a victim, then you are placing yourself in a position where you deny yourself access to the power, authority, and influence that you deserve to have. It also attracts people who are only too willing to exploit this trait. Reflect on whether this *is* what you truly want to portray. If it is not, then change your mindset and take responsibility for your thoughts and actions, to become the self-confident and powerful person you are meant to be. We all have something constructive to offer to the world, so don't expect any less of yourself. Your potential is limitless!

4. When was the last time you acted truly empathic to someone and the struggles in their life? When was the last time you looked beyond what you can see with your eyes, and asked this person what their concerns and thoughts are, and what you might do to help? It's too easy to jump to conclusions and make unfair or inaccurate judgments of others and their situations.

   Remember our previous discussions of how we can be the source of negative talk, both within ourselves and projected onto others. If you find yourself always focusing on the faults of others, or self-judging situations in an undesirable light, then pause for a moment and ask yourself this: Are you judging someone else by your own ideals in life? Are you expecting everyone else to think and do exactly as you would, and to have had the same life experiences that brought you both to this moment in life? Realize that we are all human; we all have different wants and needs, and we all struggle at different times of our lives.

5. Recognize that all of us can overreact from time to time, to get extra angry, impatient, and say or do things that are deliberately hurtful. We all know people, possibly ourselves, that will quickly explode over the smallest discrepancy or issue. Every challenge or obstacle that confronts these people becomes an excuse for actions that can be hurtful, including yelling, screaming, or hurling insults. If you find yourself quick to lose your temper, then you need to dig in and find the reason for this emotional gut response. What do you need to change about how you react or perceive difficulties? If you are the person at the receiving end of this abuse, don't accept that you deserve to receive what others dish out—want more for yourself, and follow the required steps to alter or remove yourself from these types of relationships or interactions.

6. And finally, we ALL have the ability to grow and change, at any stage or age in our lives—it is NEVER too late! There is nothing keeping us rooted in outdated thoughts or mentalities in our perceptions of ourselves, others, or the world, regarding what we feel we deserve or know we can achieve. Forgive yourself for anything you have done or allowed others to do to you, and move forward with your life. You can't change the past, but you can learn from any situation and ensure that it doesn't repeat! All you need is the willingness and bravery to take those first steps—you will be surprised at how easy it can be after that!

Moving Forward

Notice that once you identify toxic behaviors in a relationship, it is important to take the steps to eradicate them. Not only that, but it also becomes nearly impossible to pretend they are not occurring. A couple of ways you can start to uproot them is to be aware and intentional in how you respond to others and react in specific situations.

Observe how the *other* person in this toxic relationship responds back to you. Once you are aware of how this negative association functions, start identifying if there are triggers, sensitivities, or actions that create discord between you. Are both parties willing to have open communication regarding why there is an imbalance in your relationship—why there is negativity and dysfunction? Are both parties even aware of how the other person feels?

Is there an ability for a reconciliation of the relationship now that everyone's concerns have been brought to the forefront? Is there motivation on both parts to make a change? We all grow and learn as a person, so bad behaviors can be unlearned. What we are, or once were, does not have to be who we are at a future point in our life after gaining insight and the motivation for change.

Have you ever met someone who was very unkind to you at a certain time of your life, then years later, you meet them again, and they act like a totally different person? How do you react to them the second time around? Do you find yourself acting kindly to this *new* personality, or instead harshly, based on how they were before? Can you alter your perception of someone who could change, or do you hold onto the negativity of what was?

Perception in a relationship is important, and all of us have our own way of remembering words or actions, especially if you are the giver or receiver of toxicity. What we remember so clearly is unlikely how the other person will remember the same situation(s). While you're looking for an apology for previous wrongdoing, the other person may not even remember what they did to cause you any distress. Work towards embracing the positive and evolving you, as you know others can do the same. If you cannot truly forgive this person, it is okay; I won't lie and say that I've forgiven every bully from my past either. You can, however, forgive yourself and the situation that was, moving forward and away from the hurt. Shed any emotional weight that has or does still burden you.

BETRAYED – *Does she think I don't remember what she did to me? Embarrassed me in front of all my friends? They weren't even her friends; she didn't have any, so she leached off mine—but boy, she created such drama! I can't forgive her for it, yet the crazy thing is, she doesn't even remember what she did. Twenty-five years later, and I can still remember how destructive it was to several relationships I no longer have; yet to her, it barely registers as anything. Years ago, she apologized for some of the things she did, but it was too late, and my hurt was too deep. I decided it was better for me to just cut her out of my life.*

– Lynn S.

People are not perfect, and all of us have moments where we do not act in a way that reflects well on us. We might be ashamed of our behaviors or our response to the actions of others. Here are a few ways to help you during the process of changing toxic behaviors or the reactions any of us may have that are less than desirable.

Main Tips

- Establish Mental Goals – The most important thing is to set personal goals we wish to work towards. Instead of beating yourself up over previous poor behavior (either the giving or allowing yourself to receive it), start setting goals for your behavior, moving forward on a new path. No matter what, do not lose sight of the reason you are trying to change. Toxic behavior is a source of stress and unhappiness, as we have discussed in-depth, ruining the health of both ourselves and those around us, not to mention the trickledown effect to other relationships in our lives as well.

- Set Boundaries – When you start setting boundaries with yourself and what you are willing or not willing to accept, you will know if a relationship is growing. Set limitations, and measure the success of parties trying to change. Abide by what you have decided for yourself, and reinforce positive behaviors and steps ahead, without self-sabotaging progression and sliding backward. Repetition, being in tune with your feelings, and positive self-talk are key.

- Keep Active – When you make efforts to increase your activity, both physically and socially, then you are going to reap the health benefits that come from a positive mindset and attitude. Studies show that simple increases in your daily physical activity can boost your overall mental health, not to mention that being connected with happy people can reinforce what you want for yourself. Stable mental health is interconnected with good physical health and supportive social connections, not to mention improved long-term memory. Go have fun!

- Accept the Past – Part of this acceptance is not allowing your past to adversely influence your present and future behavior. It doesn't mean that you are okay with the wrongs or destructive behavior that previously happened, but it empowers you to not be weighed down by any heavy emotional burdens or guilt. Move ahead, allowing yourself to bring positivity and hope into your present and future reality.

- Be Mindful – When you are self-aware of your negative thoughts and inner dialogue, you can interrupt potential toxic thoughts and behaviors before they start to take root. You can also redirect yourself in a positive vein, as well as keeping yourself focused on the present moment. Being aware of your mindset can help hold yourself more accountable for your own behavior.

- Taking Responsibility – When you take responsibility for your actions, you are not blaming others or making excuses for your thoughts and behaviors. Owning up to your own actions can empower you to live authentically and keep you moving forward. This same mindset will also prevent you from making excuses for the behaviors of any toxic people in your life.

- Seek Support – There is a lot to be said for obtaining support from others to help you stay on the path of change. They can hold you accountable and provide a third-party viewpoint that can help you adjust your thinking from time to time. It also helps you to feel less alone as you make the effort to create real change in your life. When friendships and family are not enough, seek out professional counseling to help you through darker times, and to assist you in moving forward with new and empowering goals.

Throughout this process, it is important to remember that everything you are experiencing is a lesson that you can use to learn and grow. Recognizing and avoiding toxic behavior is critical to enjoying personal success and fulfillment in your life, while also helping you to enjoy healthy relationships. Don't be too hard on yourself for still having negative thoughts or behaviors, because if you're starting to make efforts to change, you are also now creating the solution—and it can take time.

Final Thoughts

Your life journey is full of relationships and interactions that contribute to your viewpoint, either positively or negatively. Learning to recognize the toxic attributes in relationships and encounters gives you the ability to protect your thoughts and internal dialogue. Think of how others can influence you daily. Awareness gives the power to limit those influences or shut them down altogether.

Part of what I hope you take away from this book is for you to have the power to change your circumstances, to redefine the relationships in your life or to walk away. Do not believe that what you deal with now is what you must always endure. Change is possible, but it starts with awareness. Examine your relationships, and look at them with an objective eye. If you find yourself making excuses for your behavior or someone else's, then ask yourself why.

Defining the reasons behind why you accept certain behavior, can help you better understand what has shaped you. Having that knowledge can then help you to make different choices, simply because you can better define potential triggers or the types of toxic relationships that you might be drawn to.

Now that you have started exploring what toxic relationships are, and have developed your understanding, start exploring your reactions in these relationships in a more in-depth way. Work through the steps that help improve or detangle yourself from any toxic relationships, and consider when working with a mental health professional is appropriate. Finding supportive friends and family is another way to navigate the journey of changing your toxic relationships for the better.

No matter how you choose to move forward within your situation, it is vital that you learn to provide yourself a better present and future by addressing these relationships. Do not allow any current toxicity to continue to build—this can consume you until there is nothing left of the real you.

Your life's journey should be filled with moments of peace, as well as healthy relationships that contribute to a positive environment for you to live and flourish in. May you continue to thrive in this journey of life, enjoying a path that limits the toxic elements and allows you to focus on the joy of all the different aspects of your personal journey with family and friends. I am currently developing an exciting and interactive program to guide you toward setting and implementing your personal change goals. If you feel that you want more in life, this step-by-step program is for you! Visit **Jillhartzog.com** for more information.

Want it, need it, make it happen!

About the Author

Jill Hartzog has been married for 27 years to her supportive spouse, Don. They have two children, Michael and Heather, whom they are very proud of. Jill currently lives in Ontario, Canada. She has been a registered nurse for over 29 years, working both in Canada and the US, in both hospital and home care settings.

Jill works towards her own goals, currently focusing on better health, fitness, and entrepreneurship. She has a desire to embolden women to realize and actualize their own personal and professional change goals while empowering them to stand up for themselves. For more information on her current and developing ventures, go to **Jillhartzog.com**.

Jill hopes you have found meaning, solutions, and have been inspired to continue *your* own journey of reinvention and the belief that **You Deserve More** in life. She has provided the tools to identify and understand any toxic relationships in your life and to discover options and next steps. Share what you've learned with others so that friends and family can also benefit from *their* own change goals.

Want it, need it, make it happen!

www.ingramcontent.com/pod-product-compliance
Lightning Source LLC
Chambersburg PA
CBHW060135100426
42744CB00007B/788